Maths Practice Year 3

Question Book

Sarah-Anne Fernandes

Schofield & Sims

Introduction

The **Schofield & Sims Maths Practice Year 3 Question Book** uses step-by-step practice to develop children's understanding of key mathematical concepts. It covers every Year 3 objective in the 2014 National Curriculum programme of study.

The structure

This book is split into units, which are based on the key areas of the maths curriculum for Year 3. These are:

- Number and place value
- Calculation
- Fractions
- Measurement
- Geometry
- Statistics.

Each double-page spread follows a consistent 'Practise', 'Extend' and 'Apply' sequence designed to deepen and reinforce learning. Each objective also includes a 'Remember' box that reminds children of the key information needed to help answer the questions.

At the back of the book, there is a 'Final practice' section. Here, mixed questions are used to check children's understanding of the knowledge and skills acquired throughout the book and identify any areas that need to be revisited.

A mastery approach

The **Primary Practice Maths** series follows a knowledge-based mastery approach. Children deepen their learning by applying and representing their knowledge and skills in multiple ways. This approach reinforces number concepts, nurtures fluency and strengthens both reasoning and problem-solving skills. Integral to this approach is the use of visual representations of mathematical concepts. Some of the most common visual representations used in this book are:

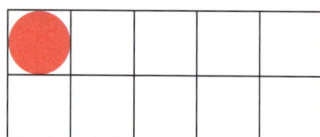

ten-frame

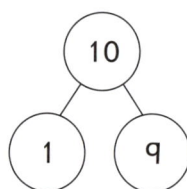

part–whole model

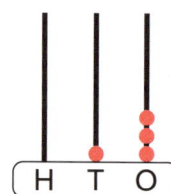

abacus

Assessment and checking progress

A 'Final practice' section is provided at the end of this book to check progress against the Year 3 maths objectives. Children are given a target time of 45 minutes to complete this section, which is marked out of 45. Once complete, it enables them to assess their new knowledge and skills independently and to see the areas where they might need more practice.

Online answers

Answers for every question in this book are available to download from the **Schofield & Sims** website. The answers are accompanied by detailed explanations where helpful. There is also a progress chart, allowing children to track their learning as they complete each set of questions, and an editable certificate.

Contents

Counting in multiples

Remember

A multiple is the result of multiplying one number by another number. 8 is a multiple of 4 and 2, because 4 × 2 = 8. 8 is also a multiple of 8 and 1 because 8 × 1 = 8. All multiples of 4 and 8 are even numbers.

Similarly, 100 is a multiple of 50 and 2 because 50 × 2 = 100. 100 is also a multiple of 100 and 1 because 100 × 1 = 100. All multiples of 50 and 100 end with a zero.

Practise

1 Find the missing multiples.

4→ **a.** 4 __8__ 12 __16__ 20 __24__ __28__ 32 __36__ 40

8→ **b.** 8 16 __24__ __32__ 40 __48__ 56 __64__ 72 __73__ __80__

50→ **c.** 50 __100__ 150 __200__ __250__ 300 __350__ __400__ 450 500

100 **d.** 100 200 __300__ 400 500 __600__ __700__ __800__ 900 __1000__

2 Write the multiple to complete the sentence.

a. The 2nd multiple of 4 is __8__.   **b.** The 4th multiple of 4 is __16__.

c. The 5th multiple of 8 is __40__.   **d.** The 7th multiple of 8 is __56__.

e. The 10th multiple of 4 is __40__.   **f.** The 10th multiple of 8 is __80__.

g. The 8th multiple of 8 is __64__.   **h.** The 6th multiple of 4 is __24__.

3 Write the multiple to complete the sentence.

a. The 3rd multiple of 50 is __150__.   **b.** The 9th multiple of 50 is __450__.

c. The 8th multiple of 100 is __800__.   **d.** The 5th multiple of 100 is __500__.

e. The 2nd multiple of 50 is __100__.   **f.** The 4th multiple of 50 is __200__.

g. The 7th multiple of 100 is __700__.   **h.** The 6th multiple of 50 is __300__.

4 Add the numbers to the Venn diagram.

| 16 | 64 | 12 | 80 | 32 | 20 | 48 |

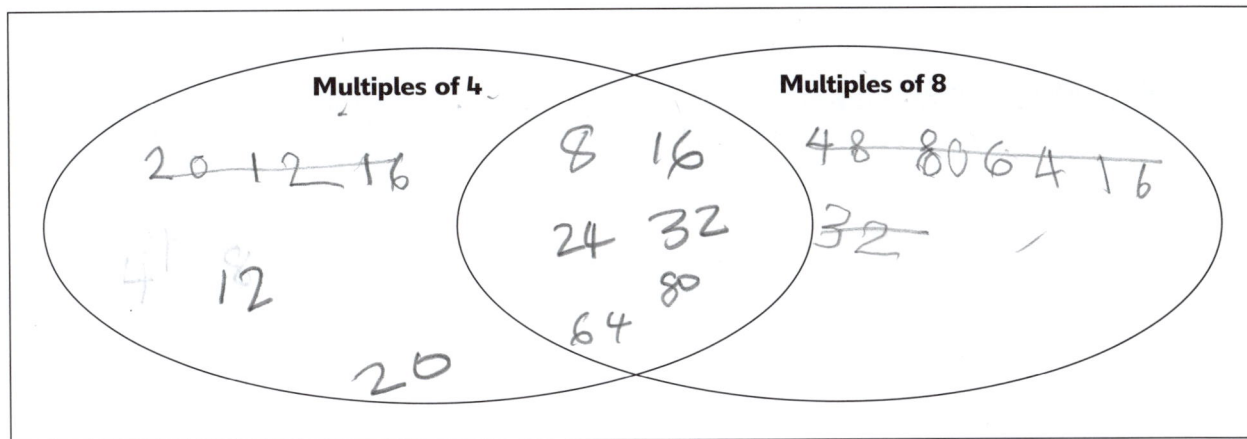

Multiples of 4 — 20 12 16   4   12   20

Multiples of 8 — (shared) 8 16 24 32 80 64

Multiples of 8 (right) — 48 80 64 16 32

5 Find the missing numbers.

a. $8 \times \underline{8} = 64$

b. $80 = \underline{8} \times 10$

c. $\underline{24} = 8 \times 3$

d. $\underline{4} \times 5 = 20$

e. $4 \times \underline{4} = 16$

f. $32 = 4 \times \underline{8}$

Apply

6 Pencils are sold in large boxes of 100 pencils and small boxes of 50 pencils. A primary school orders 7 large boxes and 5 small boxes. How many pencils have they ordered in total?

$7 \times 100 = 700$
$5 \times 50 = 250$
$700 + 250 = 950$ pencils total

7 Oliver draws a pictogram to show the number of birds that visit his bird table.

Type of bird	Number of birds
Robins	🐦 🐦 🐦 $3 \times 4 = 12$
Wrens	🐦 🐦 🐦 🐦 🐦 $4 \times 5 = 20$
Magpies	🐦 🐦 $4 \times 4 = 8$

🐦 = 4 birds

a. How many robins visited the bird table? _____ 12

b. How many more wrens than magpies visited the bird table? _____

Place value

Remember

The value of a digit depends on its position within the number. This is called its place value. For example: the three-digit number 896 is made from 8 hundreds (800) + 9 tens (90) + 6 ones (6). Breaking a number into its different parts is called partitioning.

Practise

1 Write the value of the digit 2 in each number.

   a. 402 _2 ones_ (2)   **b.** 217 _2 hundreds_ (200)   **c.** 625 _2 tens_ (20)

2 Write the value of the digit 6 in each number.

   a. 608 _6 hundred_ (600)   **b.** 763 _6 tens_ (60)   **c.** 496 _6 ones_ (6)

3 Write the value of the digit 5 in each number.

   a. 453 _5 tens_ (50)   **b.** 865 _5 ones_ (5)   **c.** 579 _5 hundreds_ (500)

4 **a.** Circle the numbers where the digit 9 has a value of nine hundred.

   90   (902)   409   195   859   (900)

   b. Circle the numbers where the digit 8 has a value of eight ones.

   780   80   (108)   897   (518)   880

5 Write the numbers in order from smallest to largest.

   a. 787   769   825   609   789

   _609 769 787 789 825_

   b. 301   325   309   387   321

   _301 309 321 325 387_

6 Find the missing numbers.

a. $567 = 500 +$ ___60___ $+ 7$

b. $785 =$ ___700___ $+ 80 + 5$

c. $8 + 60 + 100 =$ ___168___

d. $10 + 4 + 200 =$ ___2104___

7 Circle the largest number in each set.

a. 120   400   229   (480)

b. 814   329   (901)   398

c. 502   584   (587)   572

d. 345   370   378   (383)

8 Fill in the missing numbers so the numbers are in order from largest to smallest. Use each number once.

700	685	533	665

a. 675   670   _665_   655   650

b. 540   535   _533_   530   521

c. 690   689   _685_   684   680

d. 718   708   _700_   699   694

Apply

9 The bank has £100 notes, £10 notes and £1 coins. To make the amount £562 with the fewest coins and notes possible, how many £100 notes, £10 notes and £1 coins are needed?

___5___ £100 notes,   ___6___ £10 notes and   ___2___ £1 coins

10 Here is a place value chart. Two counters are missing. Write all the numbers that could have been on the place value chart.

___3 4 5 6 7 8 9___

Hundreds	Tens	Ones
●●		●

Reading and writing numbers

Remember

When reading and writing numbers in numerals and words, partition each number. A three-digit number is made up of hundreds, tens and ones. For example: 478 = 4 (hundreds) + 7 (tens) + 8 (ones) = 400 + 70 + 8. This number is written as four hundred and seventy-eight.

Practise

1 Draw lines to match each abacus to the number written in words.

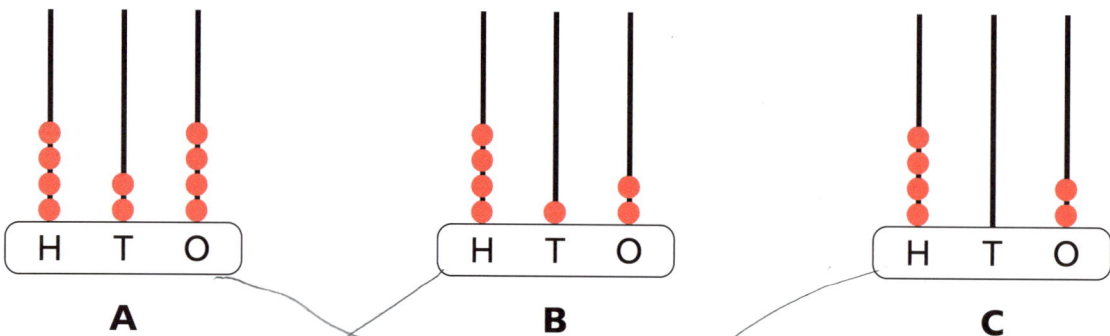

H T O	H T O	H T O
A	**B**	**C**

four hundred and twelve

four hundred and two

four hundred and twenty-four

2 Draw counters to show each number on the place value chart. Then write the number in words.

a. 418

Hundreds	Tens	Ones

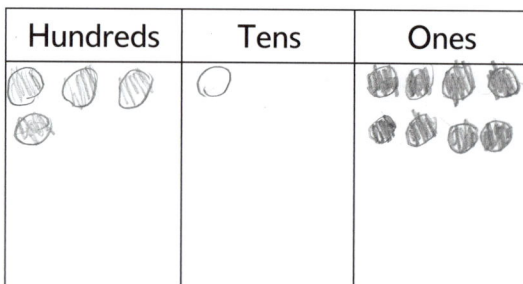

four hundred and one-eighe.

b. 643

Hundreds	Tens	Ones

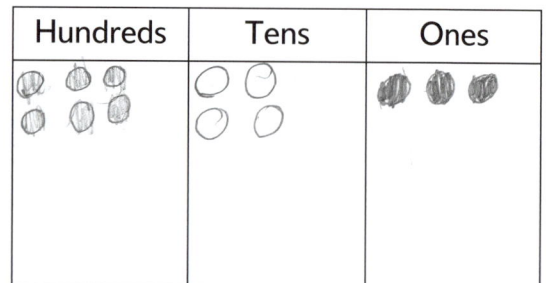

six hundred and four-three.

Tip Partition the number into hundreds, tens and ones.

3 Write the number shown by the place value counters using numerals.

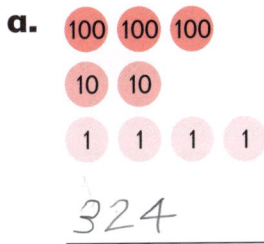

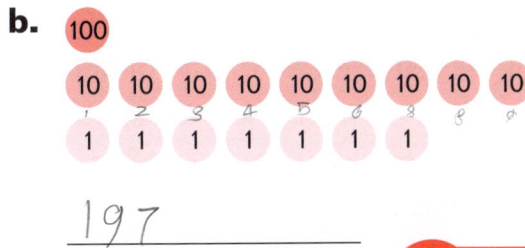

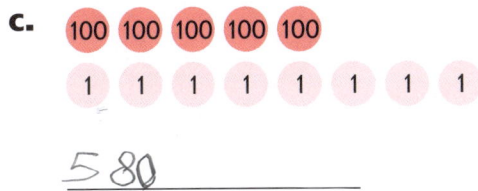

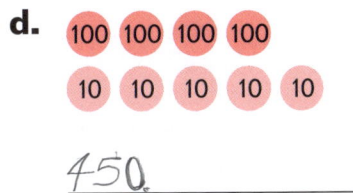

a. 100 100 100
10 10
1 1 1 1

_324_

b. 100
10 10 10 10 10 10 10 10 10
1 1 1 1 1 1 1

_197_

Tip Numerals use the digits 0, 1, 2, 3, 4, 5, 6, 7, 8 and 9.

c. 100 100 100 100 100
1 1 1 1 1 1 1 1

_580_

d. 100 100 100 100
10 10 10 10 10

_450_

4 Complete the table to show these words and numerals.

	Words	Numerals
a.	seven hundred and ninety-eight	798
b.	eight hundred and sixty-	860
c.	two hundred and fifteen	250

Apply

5 Kai rolls a die three times. He rolls a 6, a 2 and a 3. Then he makes some three-digit numbers using these numerals.

a. Write the largest even three-digit number he can make. _864_

b. Write the largest odd three-digit number he can make. _390_

c. Write the smallest even three-digit number he can make. _246_

d. Write the smallest odd three-digit number he can make. _100_

6 The cost of a camera is one hundred and forty pounds.
The cost of the camera charger is twenty-seven pounds.
Write the total cost of the camera and camera charger in digits.

_1427_

Representing numbers

Remember

A number can be represented in lots of different ways. For example: ten-frames, part–whole models, number lines, place value charts and abacuses can all be used to represent numbers.

Practise

1 Write the number shown by the place value counters.

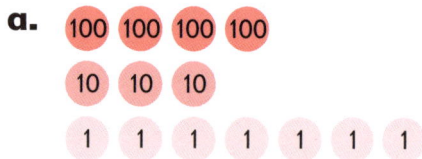

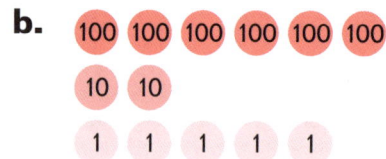

a. 100 100 100 100
10 10 10
1 1 1 1 1 1 1

_____

b. 100 100 100 100 100 100
10 10
1 1 1 1 1

_____

2 Write the number shown by each abacus.

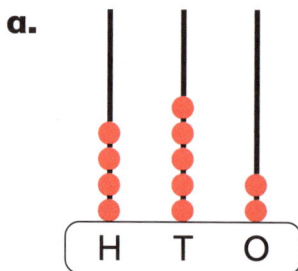

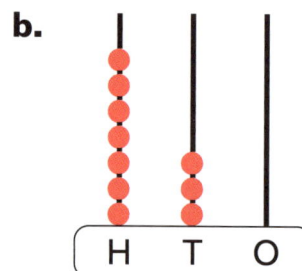

a.

H T O

_____

b.

H T O

_____

3 Complete the whole for each part–whole model.

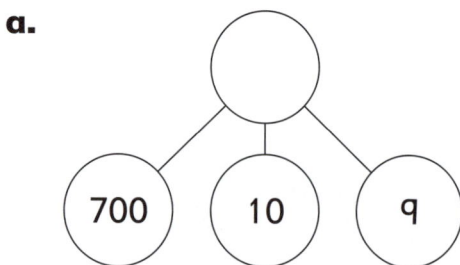

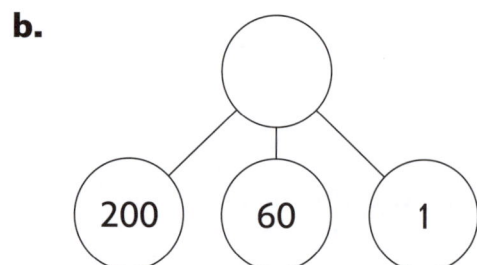

a.

700   10   9

b.

200   60   1

Tip Find the whole at the top of the part–whole model by adding together the parts at the bottom.

(4) Draw the missing counters on the place value charts to show each three-digit number.

a. 758

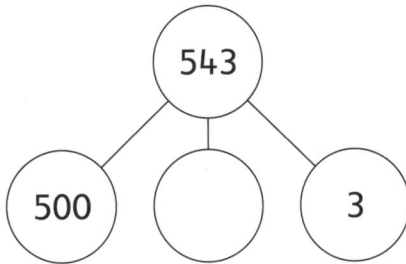

Hundreds	Tens	Ones
100 100 100	10 10 10	
100 100 100	10 10	
100		

b. 924

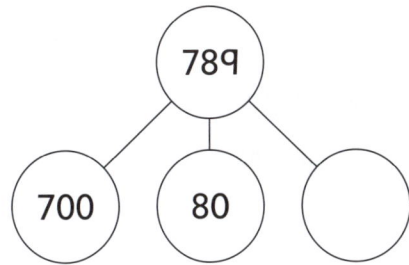

Hundreds	Tens	Ones
100 100 100		1 1 1
100 100 100		1
100 100 100		

(5) Complete the part for each part–whole model.

a.

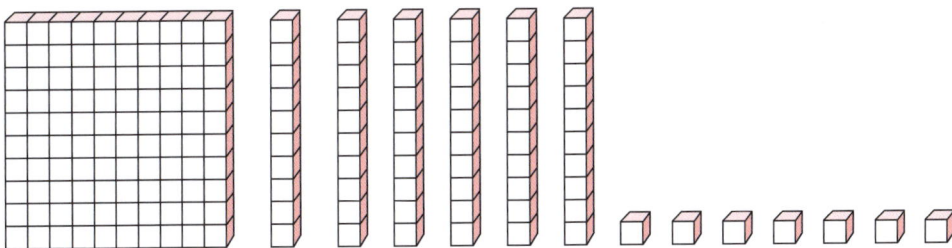

543 → 500, ( ), 3

b.

789 → 700, 80, ( )

Apply

(6) Toby represents the number 167 like this:

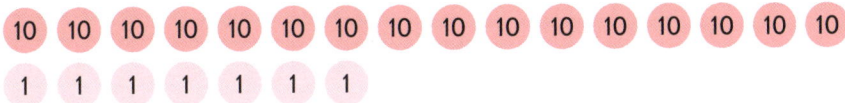

Kiran represents the same number like this:

10 10 10 10 10 10 10 10 10 10 10 10 10 10 10 10
1 1 1 1 1 1 1

Who has represented the number correctly? Circle **one**.

Toby   Kiran   Both

Explain your answer.

_____

_____

Comparing and ordering numbers

Practise

1 Here are some numbers shown using place value counters. Use the letters to order them from largest to smallest.

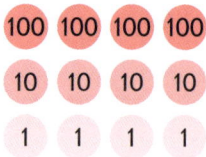

A

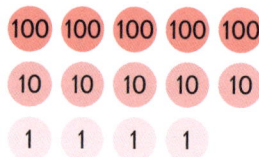

B

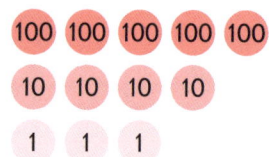

C

_____

2 Circle the larger number in each pair.

a. 678 and 891   **b.** 789 and 981   **c.** 345 and 298

d. 478 and 491   **e.** 358 and 301   **f.** 802 and 842

3 Write the correct symbol (< or >) in the circle to compare the numbers.

a. 778 ◯ 801   **b.** 674 ◯ 432   **c.** 892 ◯ 884

d. 678 ◯ 692   **e.** 258 ◯ 254   **f.** 449 ◯ 441

g. 709 ◯ 749   **h.** 863 ◯ 865   **i.** 526 ◯ 228

Tip The symbol > means 'greater than' and the symbol < means 'less than'.

④ Write these numbers in the correct position on the number line.

| 115 | 52 | 237 | 509 | 178 | 452 | 376 |

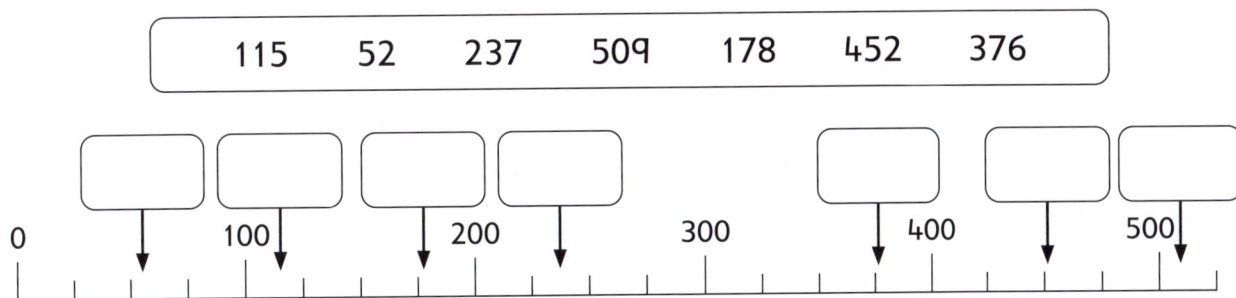

⑤ Write these numbers in order from lowest to highest.

827   890   825   614   828

_____

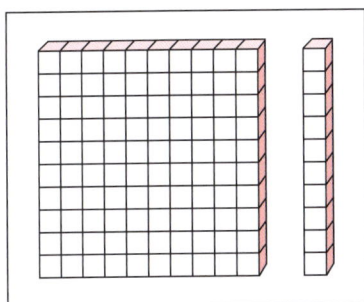 **Apply**

⑥ Davina has three number cards.

a. Write the largest number she can make.

_____

b. Write the smallest number she can make. _____

⑦ Chioma is making numbers using different representations.

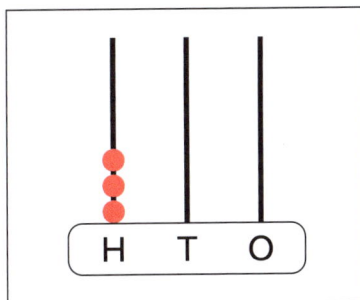

A   B   C

What is the largest number that Chioma makes? _____

Explain your answer.

_____

10 or 100 more or less

Remember

When finding 10 more or less than a number, the value of the tens digit changes. For example: $52 + 10 = 62$. The value of the tens digit has increased from 5 to 6. To add 10 to a number that already has 9 tens, exchange 10 tens for 1 hundred. For example: $94 + 10 = 104$.

To find 100 more or less than a number, change the value of the hundreds digit. For example: $552 + 100 = 652$. The value of the hundreds digit has increased from 5 to 6. To add 100 to a number that already has 9 hundreds, exchange 10 hundreds for 1 thousand. For example: $956 + 100 = 1056$.

Practise

1) Draw or cross out a bead on each abacus, then complete the sentence.

a. 10 more than 13

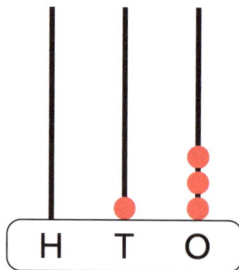

H T O

10 more than 13 is

_____.

b. 10 more than 244

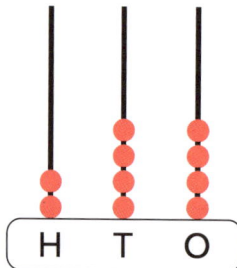

H T O

10 more than 244 is

_____.

c. 10 less than 83

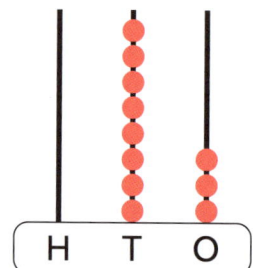

H T O

10 less than 83 is

_____.

d. 10 more than 325

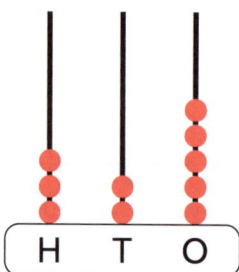

H T O

10 more than 325 is

_____.

e. 100 less than 408

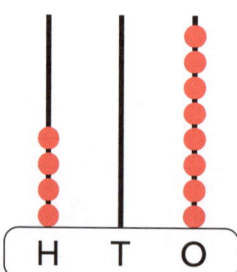

H T O

100 less than 408 is

_____.

f. 100 more than 284

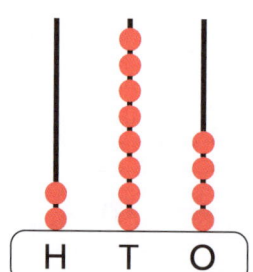

H T O

100 more than 284 is

_____.

Extend

2 Complete the table to show 10 or 100 more or less than the number.

	100 less	10 less	Number	10 more	100 more
a.			156		
b.			293		
c.			509		

3 Find the missing numbers.

a.   _____ ← 10 less **505** 10 more → _____

b.   _____ ← 10 less _____ 10 more → **107**

c.   **25** ← 10 less _____ 10 more → _____

Apply

4 Gabby has 189 stickers on her chart. She says that she will have nearly 200 when she gets 10 more. Is Gabby correct? Circle **one**.

Yes   No

Explain your answer.

_____

5 Mo has £100 in his bank account. His grandmother gives him £25. He spends £6 on a magazine and £4 on football cards. He puts the rest of the money in his bank account. How much money will he have in the bank in total?   _____

Mental addition and subtraction

Remember

When numbers are added or subtracted without a written method, it is called mental calculation. Using place value can help to add or subtract hundreds, tens or ones to or from a three-digit number.

Adding or subtracting ones will change the ones digit. For example: 634 + **2** = 636.

Adding or subtracting tens will change the tens digit. For example: 634 + **20** = 654.

Adding or subtracting hundreds will change the hundreds digit. For example: **6**34 + **200** = **8**34.

Practise

1 Calculate:

a. 345 + 3 = _____   **b.** 679 + 2 = _____   **c.** 486 + 5 = _____

d. 567 − 4 = _____   **e.** 362 − 5 = _____   **f.** 791 − 3 = _____

g. 562 + 7 = _____   **h.** 638 + 5 = _____   **i.** 804 − 8 = _____

Tip You may sometimes need to exchange 1 ten for 10 ones or 1 hundred for 10 tens.

2 Calculate:

a. 569 + 20 = _____   **b.** 208 + 80 = _____   **c.** 393 + 40 = _____

d. 498 − 30 = _____   **e.** 575 − 70 = _____   **f.** 529 − 50 = _____

g. 668 + 30 = _____   **h.** 825 − 60 = _____   **i.** 908 − 40 = _____

3 Calculate:

a. 245 + 300 = _____   **b.** 302 + 400 = _____   **c.** 834 + 300 = _____

d. 821 − 200 = _____   **e.** 628 − 500 = _____   **f.** 594 − 500 = _____

g. 486 + 500 = _____   **h.** 829 − 700 = _____   **i.** 908 − 900 = _____

4 **a.** Write these calculations in the correct part of the table.

| 568 − 9 | 566 − 3 | 563 − 7 | 565 − 2 | 591 − 8 | 588 − 4 |

No exchange of 10s	Need to exchange 10s

b. Choose **three** calculations from the table. Write the full calculation and answer for each.

_____   _____   _____

5 Complete the table to show 40 more or less than the number.

	40 less	Number	40 more
a.	613	653	
b.		722	
c.			500

Tip You might need to exchange 10 tens for 1 hundred or 1 hundred for 10 tens.

Apply

6 Solve these problems.

a. 348 children were at school on Tuesday morning. In the afternoon, 60 children in Year 3 went out on a school trip. All the other children stayed at school. How many children were at school on Tuesday afternoon?   _____

b. A school office received 168 letters over their half-term break. On Monday, 20 more letters were received. What is the total number of letters the office now has?   _____

Addition in columns

Remember

To add numbers with up to three digits, set the numbers in columns. Add the ones, then the tens and finally the hundreds. Exchange 10 ones for 1 ten, or 10 tens for 1 hundred if necessary. To estimate an answer, round the numbers before doing the calculation. Check answers using the inverse operation.

```
    2  4  5
+   1  8  2
_____
    4  2  7
    1
```

Practise

1. Draw place value counters to complete the calculations. One has been done for you.

a. 123 + 341 = _____464_____

Hundreds	Tens	Ones
100	10 10	1 1 1
100 100 100	10 10 10 10	1
100 100 100 100	10 10 10 10 10 10	1 1 1 1

b. 234 + 342 = _____

Hundreds	Tens	Ones
100 100	10 10 10	1 1 1 1
100 100 100	10 10 10 10	1 1

c. 453 + 401 = _____

Hundreds	Tens	Ones
100 100 100 100	10 10 10 10 10	1 1 1
100 100 100 100		1

d. 356 + 367 = _____

Hundreds	Tens	Ones
100 100 100	10 10 10 10 10	1 1 1 1 1 1
100 100 100	10 10 10 10 10 10	1 1 1 1 1 1 1

2 Estimate, calculate and check the answer to each calculation using the expanded column method. One calculation has been done for you.

a.
$$400 + 30 + 2$$
$$+ \ 100 + 40 + 5$$
$$\overline{ 500 + 70 + 7} \ = \ \underline{}$$

b.
$$500 + 60 + 4$$
$$+ \ 400 + 20 + 3$$
$$\overline{} \ = \ \underline{}$$

3 Estimate, calculate and check the answer to each calculation using the formal column method.

a.
$$\begin{array}{r} 2\ 2\ 6 \\ +\ 3\ 5\ 3 \\ \hline \\ \hline \end{array}$$

b.
$$\begin{array}{r} 4\ 5\ 3 \\ +\ 5\ 4\ 5 \\ \hline \\ \hline \end{array}$$

4 Complete these calculations using the expanded or formal column method.

a. 427 + 244 = _____

b. 342 + 93 = _____

Apply

5 Fill in the missing digits to complete the calculation.

a.
$$\begin{array}{r} 1\ 8\ 6 \\ +\ 3\ \boxed{}\ \boxed{} \\ \hline 4\ 9\ 8 \\ \hline \end{array}$$

b.
$$\begin{array}{r} 1\ 8\ 4 \\ +\ 9\ \boxed{}\ \boxed{} \\ \hline \boxed{}\ 0\ 9\ 3 \\ \hline \end{array}$$

6 Solve these problems.

a. Red class earned 258 stars in the autumn term. They increase their stars by 273 in the spring term. How many stars do they have? _____

b. Kim uses 275g of seeds to feed her hamster and 445g of seeds to feed her guinea pigs each week. What is the total amount of seeds that she uses each week to feed her pets? _____

c. There are 458 cola cans, 276 lemonade cans and 134 orange cans. How many cans are there altogether? _____

Remember

When subtracting numbers with up to three digits, set the numbers into columns. First, subtract the ones, then the tens and finally the hundreds. Sometimes it is necessary to exchange 1 ten for 10 ones, or 1 hundred for 10 tens. To estimate an answer, round the numbers before doing the calculation. Check answers using the inverse operation. Addition and subtraction are inverse operations.

$$\begin{array}{r} {}^{1}\;2\;{}^{1}4\;\;5 \\ -\;\;1\;\;8\;\;2 \\ \hline 6\;\;3 \end{array}$$

Practise

1 Cross off the place value counters to subtract the numbers and draw any exchanged counters needed. Then write the answer in digits. One has been done for you.

a. 563 − 342 = ___221___

Hundreds	Tens	Ones
100 100 100	10 10 10	1 1 1
100 100	10 10 10	

b. 784 − 251 = _____

Hundreds	Tens	Ones
100 100 100	10 10 10	1 1 1
100 100 100	10 10 10	1
100	10 10	

c. 482 − 135 = _____

Hundreds	Tens	Ones
100 100 100	10 10 10	1 1
100	10 10 10	
	10 10	

d. 364 − 129 = _____

Hundreds	Tens	Ones
100 100 100	10 10 10	1 1 1
	10 10 10	1

e. 628 − 243 = _____

Hundreds	Tens	Ones
100 100 100	10 10	1 1 1
100 100 100		1 1 1
		1 1

f. 807 − 267 = _____

Hundreds	Tens	Ones
100 100 100		1 1 1
100 100 100		1 1 1
100 100		1

2 Estimate, calculate and check the answer to each calculation using the expanded column method. One calculation has been done for you.

a. $500 + 60 + 8$

$- 300 + 30 + 2$

$\textcolor{red}{200 + 30 + 6}$ = _____

b. $400 + 40 + 5$

$- 200 + 10 + 3$

 = _____

3 Estimate, calculate and check the answer to each calculation using the formal column method.

a. $9 6 8$

$- 6 5 4$

_____

b. $8 4 3$

$- 5 1 2$

_____

4 Complete these calculations using the expanded or formal column method.

a. $456 - 324 =$ _____

b. $549 - 76 =$ _____

Apply

5 Fill in the missing digits to complete the calculation.

a. $3 6 9$

$- 2 \boxed{} 5$

$1 4 \boxed{}$

b. $4 \boxed{} 6$

$- \boxed{} 3 \boxed{}$

$2 2 8$

6 Solve these problems.

a. The cost of a microwave was £378. The price decreases by £125. How much is the microwave now? _____

b. There were 672 people at a concert. 285 people left the concert at 10 p.m. How many people stayed at the concert? _____

c. The table shows the heights of two buildings. What is the difference between the heights of the two buildings?

Tower 72	The Big Bertie
278m	302m

_____

Mental multiplication and division

Numbers can be multiplied and divided without a written method. This is called mental calculation. Learning the 2, 3, 4, 5, 8 and 10 times tables will help with recalling multiplication facts quickly when calculating.

Division is the inverse operation of multiplication, so multiplication facts can be useful to help with division facts. For example: $3 \times 6 = 18$ so $18 \div 3 = 6$.

Practise

1) Complete the calculations using the three times table.

a. $3 \times 1 =$ _____

b. $3 \times 3 =$ _____

c. $3 \times 8 =$ _____

d. $3 \times 11 =$ _____

e. $30 \div 3 =$ _____

f. $24 \div 3 =$ _____

g. $12 \div 3 =$ _____

h. $36 \div 3 =$ _____

i. $3 \times$ _____ $= 27$

j. $3 \times$ _____ $= 15$

k. _____ $= 3 \times 2$

l. _____ $= 21 \div 3$

2) Complete the calculations using the four times table.

a. $4 \times 2 =$ _____

b. $4 \times 4 =$ _____

c. $4 \times 0 =$ _____

d. $4 \times 8 =$ _____

e. $44 \div 4 =$ _____

f. $24 \div 4 =$ _____

g. $4 \div 4 =$ _____

h. $36 \div 4 =$ _____

i. $4 \times$ _____ $= 48$

j. $4 \times$ _____ $= 12$

k. _____ $= 4 \times 10$

l. _____ $= 28 \div 4$

3) Complete the calculations using the eight times table.

a. $8 \times 2 =$ _____

b. $8 \times 3 =$ _____

c. $8 \times 10 =$ _____

d. $8 \times 8 =$ _____

e. $32 \div 8 =$ _____

f. $96 \div 8 =$ _____

g. $56 \div 8 =$ _____

h. $40 \div 8 =$ _____

i. $8 \times$ _____ $= 24$

j. $8 \times$ _____ $= 16$

k. _____ $= 8 \times 11$

l. _____ $= 48 \div 8$

(4) Write the missing numbers to complete the multiplications squares. One number has been done for you.

a.

×	3	4	8
2		8	
5	15		40
8		32	

b.

×	6	5	7
	48	40	
3		15	
10	60	50	

(5) Use the multiplication facts to find the missing numbers.

a. $3 \times 8 = 24$ $3 \times \underline{\hspace{2cm}} = 240$ $240 \div \underline{\hspace{2cm}} = 3$

b. $9 \times 4 = 36$ $\underline{\hspace{2cm}} \times 40 = 360$ $360 \div \underline{\hspace{2cm}} = 9$

c. $8 \times 8 = 64$ $\underline{\hspace{2cm}} \times 8 = 640$ $640 \div 8 = \underline{\hspace{2cm}}$

Apply

(6) Solve these problems.

a. Here are some boxes and bags with balls in them. Are there more balls in the boxes or in the bags? Circle **one**.

Boxes

Bags

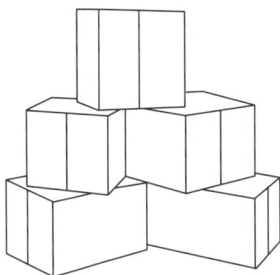

30 balls in each box

20 balls in each bag

b. 560 tins of soup are packed into 8 boxes. How many tins of soup are put into each box? _____

Written multiplication and division

Remember

Multiplication and division calculations can be completed using partitioning. Partitioning means separating a number according to its place value. For example: 72 = 70 + 2. Partition two-digit numbers into tens and ones and then multiply or divide each by a one-digit number.

Practise

1 Complete these part–whole models for multiplication. One has been done for you.

a.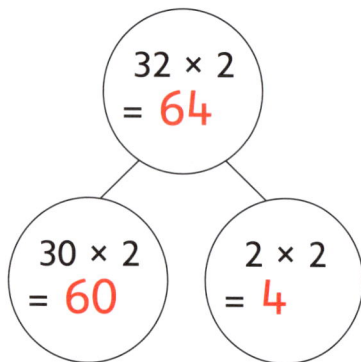

b.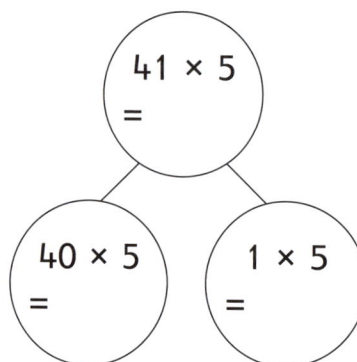

c.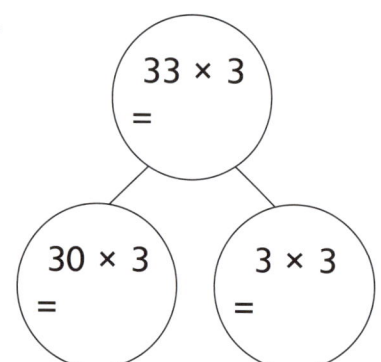

Tip Remember to use times tables and division facts to answer multiplication and division problems.

2 a. Use the place value counters to divide 68 into 2 equal groups.

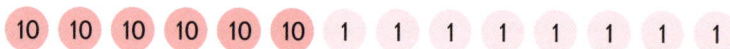

What is the value of the counters in each group?

_____

b. Use the place value counters to divide 96 into 3 equal groups.

What is the value of the counters in each group? _____

3 Calculate:

a. 31 × 4 = _____

b. 42 × 4 = _____

c. 21 × 8 = _____

d. 22 × 3 = _____

e. 34 × 3 = _____

f. 46 × 3 = _____

g. 54 × 4 = _____

h. 58 × 3 = _____

i. 74 × 8 = _____

j. 63 × 4 = _____

4 Calculate:

a. 69 ÷ 3 = _____

b. 84 ÷ 4 = _____

c. 66 ÷ 2 = _____

d. 93 ÷ 3 = _____

e. 92 ÷ 4 = _____

f. 87 ÷ 3 = _____

g. 76 ÷ 4 = _____

h. 54 ÷ 3 = _____

Apply

5 Calculate the remainder for each division problem.

a. 19 eggs packed into boxes of 6 eggs. The remainder is _____ eggs.

b. 27 apples packed into bags of 5 apples. The remainder is _____ apples.

c. 42 cans packed into packs of 4 cans. The remainder is _____ cans.

Tip The remainder is the amount left over once the calculation is complete.

6 Tessa is making gingerbread biscuits. The recipe makes six biscuits. Tessa wants to make 24 gingerbread biscuits. Write how much she needs of each ingredient.

brown sugar: _____   plain flour: _____

ginger: _____   butter: _____

Gingerbread recipe

80g brown sugar
120g plain flour
2 tsp ginger
60g butter

Multiplication and division word problems

Practise

1 Solve these multiplication word problems.

a. Bananas are sold in bunches of 6.

How many bananas are in 9 bunches? _____

b. What is the product of 9 and 8? _____

c. There are 7 groups of children doing art. Each group has
8 children. How many children are doing art altogether? _____

2 Solve these division word problems.

a. Cupcakes are sold in boxes of 4. Alice's mum buys
16 cupcakes for Alice's birthday. How many boxes
of cupcakes does Alice's mum buy? _____

b. Here is a balance scale with four boxes on one side and a 96kg weight on the
other side. What is the mass of each box if each box has the same mass?

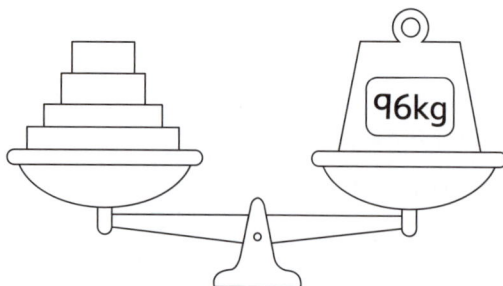

96kg

_____

c. Maxine spends £84 on books. Each book costs £3.
How many books does Maxine buy? _____

3 Solve these problems.

a. Sheila has 12 jars of biscuits. 8 jars have 6 biscuits in, and 4 jars have 8 biscuits in. How many biscuits are there in total? _____

b. The park café sells 43 cans of drink on Friday. On Saturday, it sells 5 times as many cans of drinks as on Friday. On Sunday, it sells 3 times as many cans of drinks as on Friday. How many cans of drinks does the park café sell in total on Saturday and Sunday? _____

Apply

4 Jack goes out for Sunday lunch. He chooses one roast and two different vegetables.

Roast: chicken, lamb or nut loaf   Vegetables: carrots, peas or beans

a. List all the different meals he can choose from the menu.

Roast	Vegetable	Vegetable

b. How many different combinations of lunch can Jack have? _____

Tenths

Remember

One tenth is 1 of 10 equal parts. One tenth is written as $\frac{1}{10}$.

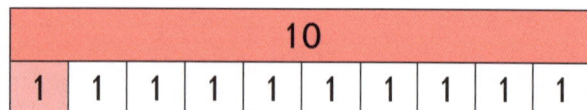

Three tenths are 3 of 10 equal parts. Three tenths are written as $\frac{3}{10}$.

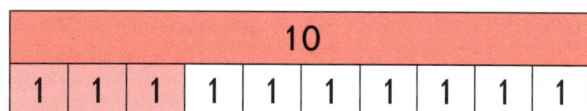

To find a tenth of a number, divide the whole by 10. For example: one tenth of 50 is $50 \div 10 = 5$.

Practise

1 Write the fraction of each diagram that is shaded.

a.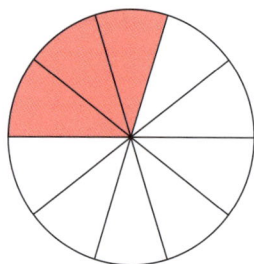

b.

c.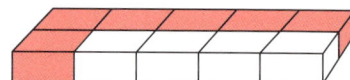

_____   _____   _____

2 Write the missing tenths in these sequences.

a. $\frac{2}{10}$ $\frac{3}{10}$ _____ $\frac{5}{10}$ $\frac{6}{10}$ _____ $\frac{8}{10}$

b. $1\frac{4}{10}$ $1\frac{5}{10}$ _____ $1\frac{7}{10}$ $1\frac{8}{10}$ $1\frac{9}{10}$ _____

c. $5\frac{3}{10}$ $5\frac{2}{10}$ $5\frac{1}{10}$ _____   _____ $4\frac{8}{10}$ $4\frac{7}{10}$

» Extend

3 Write the missing number in each part–whole model. The sum of the fractions at the bottom must equal the fraction at the top.

a.

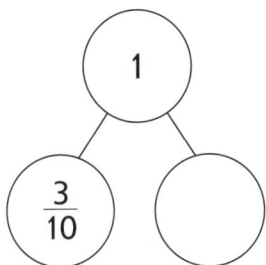

b.

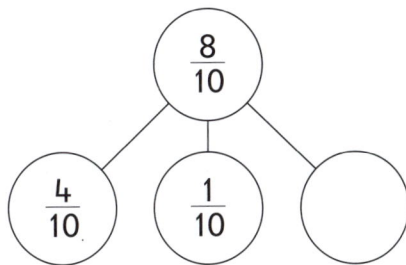

c.

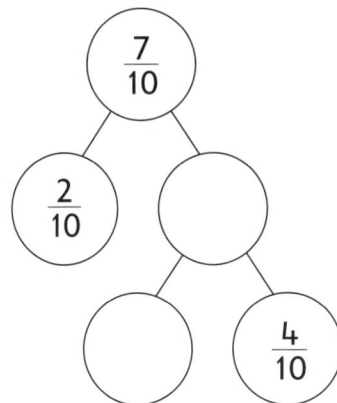

> **Tip** When adding fractions together, only add the top numbers (numerators) together.

4 Calculate:

a. $4 \div 10 = \dfrac{}{10}$

b. $6 \div 10 = \dfrac{}{10}$

c. $9 \div 10 = \dfrac{}{10}$

d. $5 \div 10 = \dfrac{}{10}$

e. $\underline{} \div 10 = \dfrac{2}{10}$

f. $7 \div \underline{} = \dfrac{7}{10}$

g. $\underline{} \div 10 = \dfrac{1}{10}$

h. $3 \div 10 = \underline{}$

i. $8 \div \underline{} = \dfrac{8}{10}$

Apply

5 A small fruit salad bowl has a total of ten chunks of fruit. $\frac{2}{10}$ of the fruit salad is pineapple. $\frac{4}{10}$ of the fruit salad is grape. The rest of the fruit salad is melon. What fraction of the fruit salad is melon? $\underline{}$

6 Neema is wrapping presents. She uses $\frac{2}{10}$ of a metre of ribbon for every present. How many presents can she wrap using a 5m ball of ribbon? Use the bar model to help.

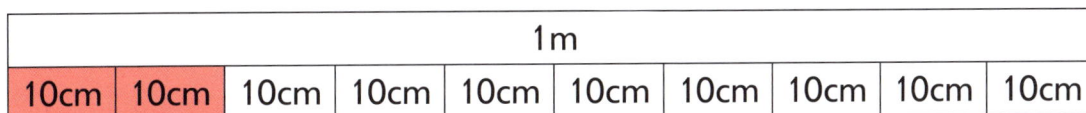

$\underline{}$

Finding fractions of a number

A fraction is part of a whole. To find a fraction of a number or quantity, divide the whole by the denominator to find one equal part, then multiply by the numerator.

For example: to calculate $\frac{2}{3}$ of 15, divide the whole number (15) by the denominator (3), then multiply by the numerator (2) to find two parts.

$15 \div 3 = 5$ 5 is $\frac{1}{3}$ of 15 $5 \times 2 = 10$ 10 is $\frac{2}{3}$ of 15

Practise

1 Find the fraction of each amount.

a. Circle $\frac{1}{2}$ of the strawberries.

b. Circle $\frac{2}{3}$ of the pencils.

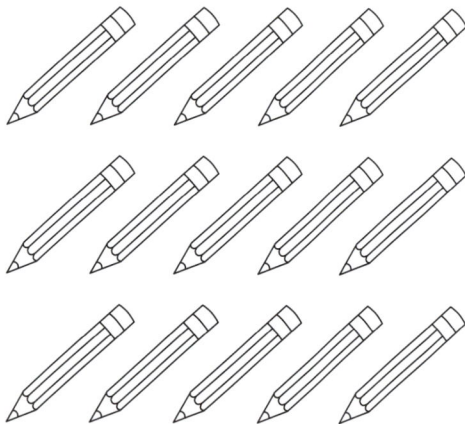

c. Circle $\frac{3}{4}$ of the marbles.

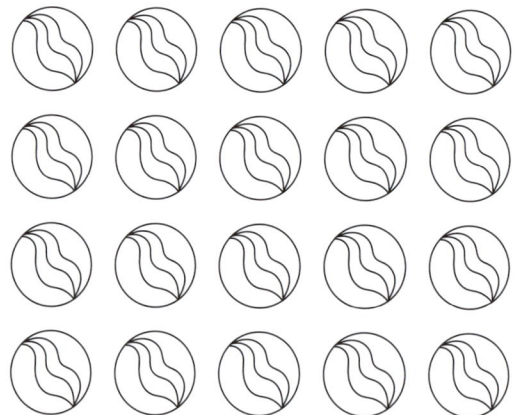

2 Use the bar diagram to find the fractions of 24.

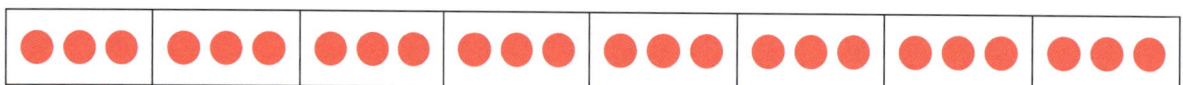

a. $\frac{1}{8}$ of 24 = _____

b. $\frac{2}{8}$ of 24 = _____

c. $\frac{5}{8}$ of 24 = _____

» Extend

3 Write the missing number in each unshaded bar. One has been done for you.

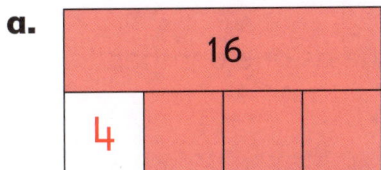

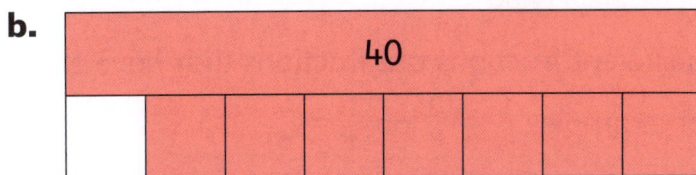

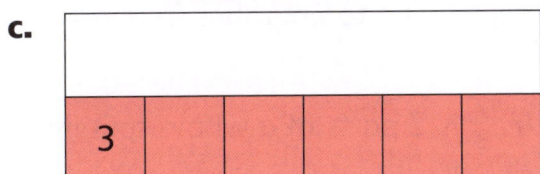

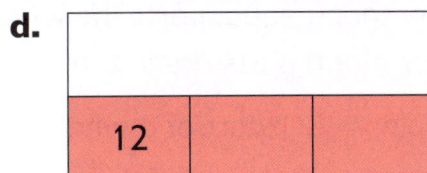

a.

16			
4			

b.

40						

c.

3				

d.

12		

4 Find the fractions of each amount.

a. $\frac{1}{10}$ of 30 = _____   **b.** $\frac{1}{5}$ of 25 = _____   **c.** $\frac{1}{4}$ of 32 = _____

d. $\frac{4}{10}$ of 30 = _____   **e.** $\frac{2}{5}$ of 25 = _____   **f.** $\frac{3}{4}$ of 36 = _____

Apply

5 Ben and Sara do a maths quiz. Ben scored $\frac{4}{5}$ out of 60 marks. Sara scored $\frac{2}{3}$ out of 60 marks. Who scored the most marks? Circle **one**.

Ben   Sara

Explain your answer.

_____

6 Arjun draws circles, squares and triangles on a grid.

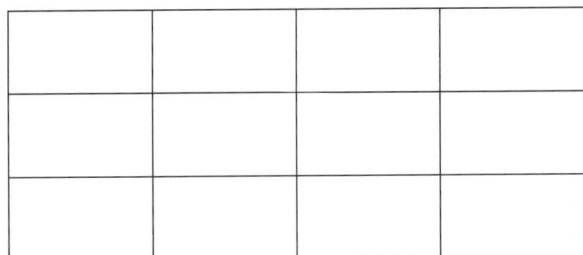

Tip Draw the shapes on the grid to solve the problem.

$\frac{2}{3}$ of the grid is covered with squares. $\frac{1}{4}$ of the grid is covered with triangles. The rest of the grid is covered with circles. What fraction of the grid is covered with circles? _____

Equivalent fractions

Chapter 3

Remember

Equivalent fractions are fractions that have the same value as one another.

For example: $\frac{1}{4} = \frac{2}{8}$ or $\frac{2}{3} = \frac{4}{6}$.

Remember that a fraction is part of a whole. The bottom number (denominator) shows how many equal parts the whole is split into. The top number (numerator) shows how many parts are in the fraction.

For example: $\frac{1}{4}$ is 1 part of a whole split into 4. $\frac{2}{8}$ is 2 parts of a whole split into 8.

Practise

1. Use the bars to find the equivalent fraction and fill in the missing numbers.

   a. $\frac{1}{4} = \frac{}{8}$
   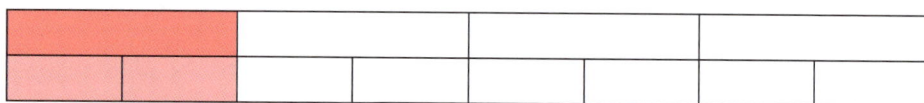

   b. $\frac{2}{3} = \underline{}$
   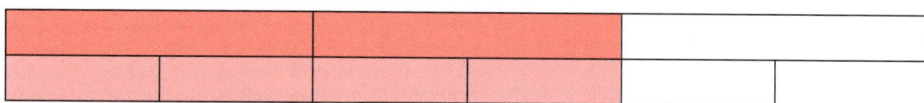

   c. $\frac{4}{10} = \underline{}$
   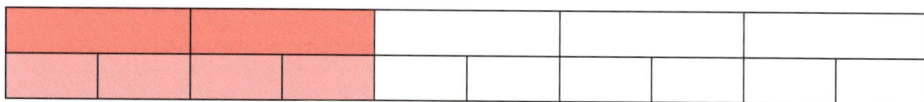

2. Shade the bar to show each equivalent fraction and fill in the missing numbers.

   a. $\frac{2}{3} = \frac{4}{} = \frac{}{12}$

   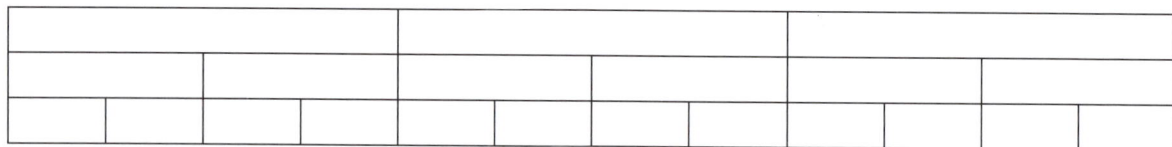

   b. $\frac{3}{5} = \frac{}{10} = \frac{}{20}$

   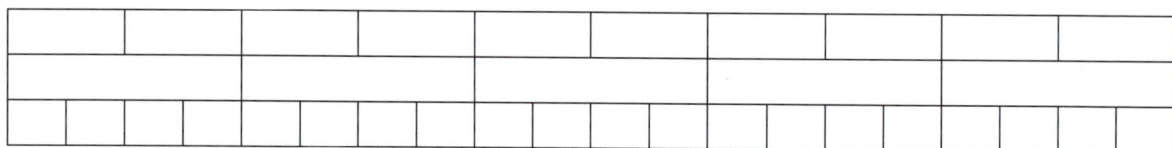

≫ Extend

3 Use the fraction wall to complete the fraction statements.

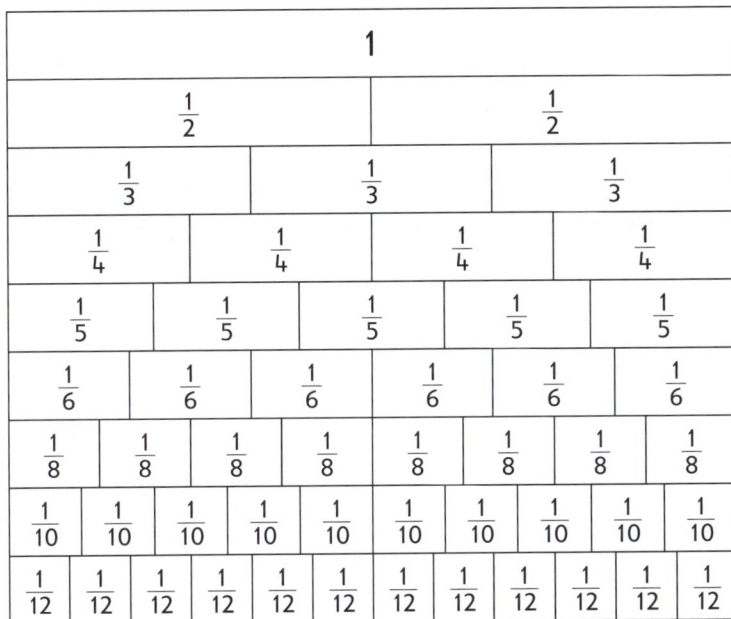

> **Tip** The fraction wall shows unit fractions. A unit fraction is any fraction with 1 as the numerator. The denominator is any positive whole number. It shows the number of equal parts the whole has been split into.

a. $\dfrac{1}{2} = \dfrac{}{6} = \dfrac{}{12}$

b. $\dfrac{1}{3} = \dfrac{}{6} = \dfrac{}{12}$

c. $\dfrac{5}{10} = \dfrac{2}{} = \dfrac{3}{}$

d. $\dfrac{3}{4} = \dfrac{}{8} = \dfrac{}{12}$

4 Tick the diagrams that show a fraction equivalent to $\dfrac{3}{4}$.

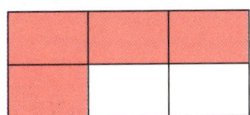   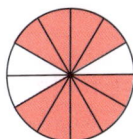   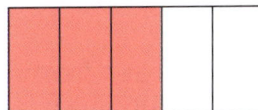   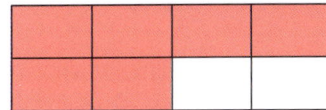

A ☐   B ☐   C ☐   D ☐

☁ Apply

5 Indira has been making equivalent fraction pairs.

$\dfrac{2}{3} = \dfrac{4}{6}$ $\dfrac{1}{5} = \dfrac{2}{10}$ $\dfrac{3}{4} = \dfrac{6}{8}$

She says that she has spotted a pattern to make equivalent fractions. Describe a pattern for making these equivalent fractions.

_____

Comparing and ordering fractions

Remember

When comparing fractions with the same denominator, look at the numerator. For example: $\frac{2}{5}$ is smaller than $\frac{4}{5}$ because 2 is smaller than 4.

When comparing fractions with different denominators, such as $\frac{2}{5}$ and $\frac{5}{10}$, use a fraction wall to see which fraction takes up more space and is larger.

Practise

1 Write the correct symbol (< or >) in the circle to compare these fractions. One has been done for you.

a. $\frac{1}{4}$ $<$ $\frac{3}{4}$

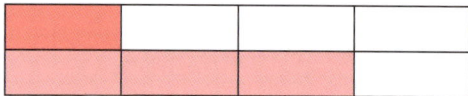

b. $\frac{2}{3}$ ◯ $\frac{1}{3}$

c. $\frac{4}{10}$ ◯ $\frac{8}{10}$

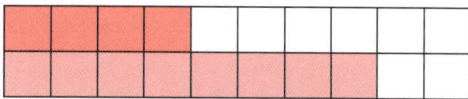

d. $\frac{4}{5}$ ◯ $\frac{2}{5}$

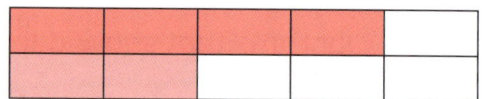

2 Write the shaded fractions in order from smallest to largest.

a.

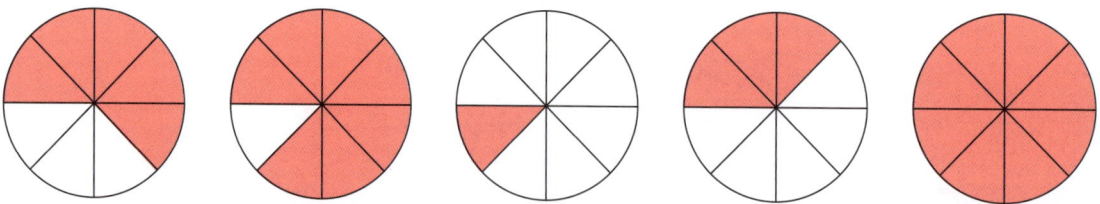

b.

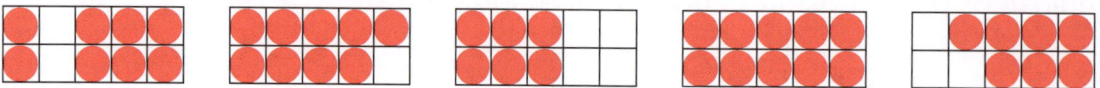

Tip **Question 2b** uses ten-frames. Each whole frame has been split into tenths.

3 Write whether the number statements are true or false.

a. $\frac{1}{10}$ is larger than $\frac{1}{8}$.

_____

b. $\frac{1}{6}$ is smaller than $\frac{1}{4}$.

_____

c. $\frac{1}{3}$ is larger than $\frac{1}{4}$.

_____

d. $\frac{1}{8}$ is smaller than $\frac{1}{5}$.

_____

1									
$\frac{1}{2}$					$\frac{1}{2}$				
$\frac{1}{3}$			$\frac{1}{3}$			$\frac{1}{3}$			
$\frac{1}{4}$		$\frac{1}{4}$		$\frac{1}{4}$		$\frac{1}{4}$			
$\frac{1}{5}$		$\frac{1}{5}$		$\frac{1}{5}$		$\frac{1}{5}$		$\frac{1}{5}$	
$\frac{1}{6}$		$\frac{1}{6}$	$\frac{1}{6}$		$\frac{1}{6}$		$\frac{1}{6}$		$\frac{1}{6}$
$\frac{1}{8}$	$\frac{1}{8}$	$\frac{1}{8}$	$\frac{1}{8}$	$\frac{1}{8}$	$\frac{1}{8}$	$\frac{1}{8}$	$\frac{1}{8}$		
$\frac{1}{10}$	$\frac{1}{10}$	$\frac{1}{10}$	$\frac{1}{10}$	$\frac{1}{10}$	$\frac{1}{10}$	$\frac{1}{10}$	$\frac{1}{10}$	$\frac{1}{10}$	$\frac{1}{10}$

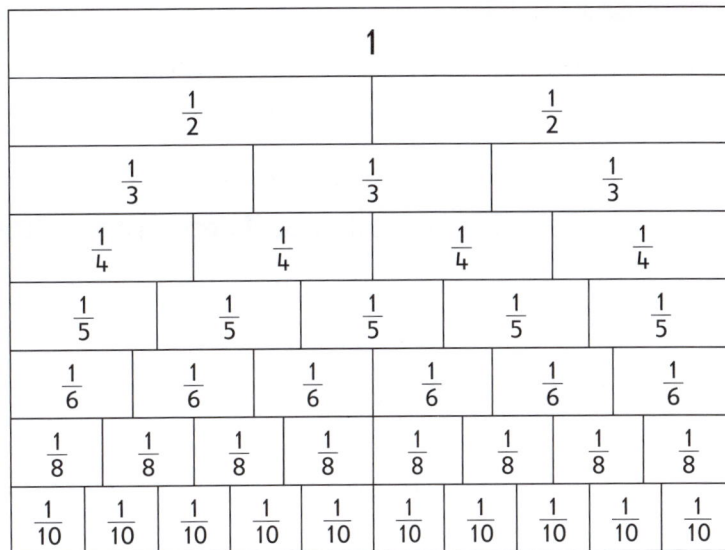

4 Circle the largest fraction in each set.

a. $\frac{1}{5}$ $\frac{1}{12}$ $\frac{1}{3}$ $\frac{1}{2}$

b. $\frac{1}{10}$ $\frac{1}{3}$ $\frac{1}{4}$ $\frac{1}{6}$

c. $\frac{1}{20}$ $\frac{1}{8}$ $\frac{1}{10}$ $\frac{1}{2}$

5 Write the fractions in the correct set.

$$\frac{1}{2} \quad \frac{3}{5} \quad \frac{1}{12} \quad \frac{1}{4} \quad \frac{1}{10}$$

Greater than $\frac{1}{5}$	**Less than $\frac{1}{8}$**

Apply

6 Mia, Iona and Andrea each have a sandwich. Mia cuts her sandwich into quarters. Iona cuts her sandwich into thirds. Andrea cuts her sandwich into halves. Who cuts their sandwich into the smallest pieces?

_____

Adding fractions

Remember

When two fractions are added, the denominator stays the same and only the top numbers (numerators) are added together. For example: $\frac{2}{6} + \frac{4}{6} = \frac{6}{6} = 1$.

This calculation can be shown using a bar model.
The shaded and unshaded parts equal the whole ($\frac{6}{6}$).

Practise

1 Use the images to add the fractions and fill in the missing numbers.

a.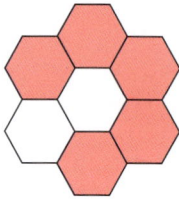

b.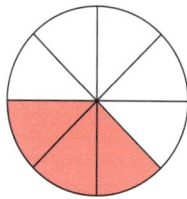

c.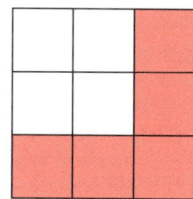

$$\frac{}{7} + \frac{}{7} = \frac{7}{7} \qquad \frac{}{8} + \frac{}{8} = \frac{8}{8} \qquad \frac{}{9} + \frac{}{9} = 1$$

2 Complete the calculations using the fraction bars.

a. $\frac{2}{5} + \frac{1}{5} = \frac{}{5}$

b. $\frac{3}{10} + \frac{4}{10} = \frac{}{10}$

c. $\frac{1}{4} + \frac{1}{4} = \underline{}$

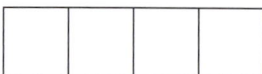

d. $\frac{2}{7} + \frac{3}{7} = \underline{}$

3 Complete these calculations using the number lines.

a. $\frac{1}{5} + \frac{3}{5} = \underline{}$

b. $\frac{3}{9} + \frac{2}{9} + \frac{1}{9} = \underline{}$

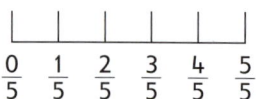

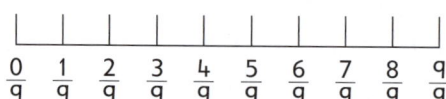

4. Add the shaded fractions shown in the circles.

a.

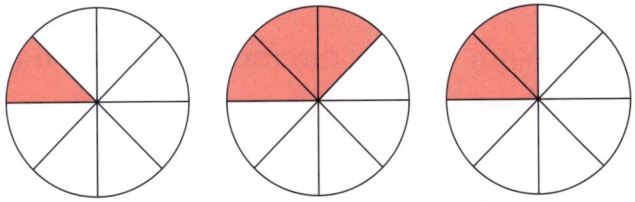

_____

b.

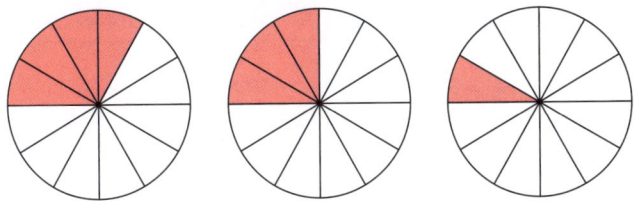

_____

5. Tick to show whether the calculations are true or false.

		True	False
a.	$\frac{1}{3} + \frac{2}{3} = 1$		
b.	$\frac{4}{7} + \frac{2}{7} < 1$		
c.	$\frac{5}{8} + \frac{4}{8} < 1$		
d.	$\frac{4}{10} + \frac{4}{10} < 1$		

Tip If the numerator is greater than the denominator when the fractions have been added, the fraction is greater than one whole.

Apply

6. On Saturday, Max read $\frac{3}{10}$ of his book. On Sunday, he read $\frac{5}{10}$ more. On Monday, Max reached the end of the book. What fraction of the book did Max read on Monday? _____

7. Find the missing numbers.

a. ★ $= \frac{1}{6} + \frac{1}{6}$ ● $= \frac{2}{6} + \frac{1}{6}$ b. ⬠ $= \frac{2}{8} + \frac{3}{8}$ ◆ $= \frac{4}{8} + \frac{2}{8}$

★ + ● = _____

◆ + ⬠ = _____

Subtracting fractions

Remember

When you subtract fractions, the denominator stays the same and only the top numbers (numerators) subtract. For example: $\frac{6}{6} - \frac{2}{6} = \frac{4}{6}$.

This calculation can be shown using a bar model.
Subtract the shaded parts ($\frac{2}{6}$) from the whole ($\frac{6}{6}$) to get the unshaded part ($\frac{4}{6}$).

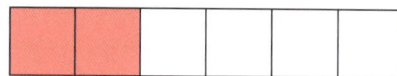

Practise

1. Complete these calculations using the number line.

   a. $\frac{6}{6} - \frac{2}{6} =$ _____

   $\frac{0}{6} \quad \frac{1}{6} \quad \frac{2}{6} \quad \frac{3}{6} \quad \frac{4}{6} \quad \frac{5}{6} \quad \frac{6}{6}$

   b. $\frac{8}{9} - \frac{3}{9} =$ _____

   $\frac{0}{9} \quad \frac{1}{9} \quad \frac{2}{9} \quad \frac{3}{9} \quad \frac{4}{9} \quad \frac{5}{9} \quad \frac{6}{9} \quad \frac{7}{9} \quad \frac{8}{9} \quad \frac{9}{9}$

   c. $\frac{5}{8} - \frac{2}{8} =$ _____

   $\frac{0}{8} \quad \frac{1}{8} \quad \frac{2}{8} \quad \frac{3}{8} \quad \frac{4}{8} \quad \frac{5}{8} \quad \frac{6}{8} \quad \frac{7}{8} \quad \frac{8}{8}$

   d. $\frac{5}{10} - \frac{3}{10} =$ _____

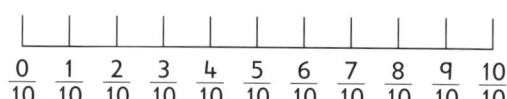

   $\frac{0}{10} \quad \frac{1}{10} \quad \frac{2}{10} \quad \frac{3}{10} \quad \frac{4}{10} \quad \frac{5}{10} \quad \frac{6}{10} \quad \frac{7}{10} \quad \frac{8}{10} \quad \frac{9}{10} \quad \frac{10}{10}$

2. Finley has some bead strings.

   a. The first bead string has 10 beads.

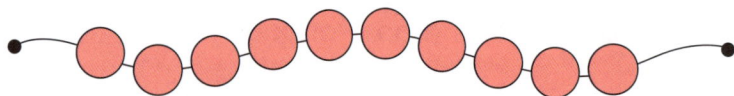

   4 beads fall off. What fraction of the original beads are left? _____

   b. The second bead string has 12 beads.

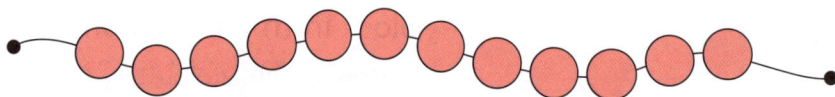

   5 beads fall off. What fraction of the original beads are left? _____

3 Calculate:

a. $\dfrac{10}{11} - \dfrac{4}{11} =$ _____

b. $\dfrac{8}{12} - \dfrac{3}{12} =$ _____

c. $\dfrac{3}{4} - \dfrac{1}{4} =$ _____

d. $\dfrac{9}{10} - \dfrac{2}{10} =$ _____

e. $\dfrac{5}{8} - \dfrac{3}{8} =$ _____

f. $\dfrac{4}{5} - \dfrac{1}{5} =$ _____

4 Calculate the difference between each pair of fractions.

a. $\dfrac{1}{5}$ and $\dfrac{2}{5}$ _____

b. $\dfrac{2}{8}$ and $\dfrac{6}{8}$ _____

c. $\dfrac{4}{20}$ and $\dfrac{10}{20}$ _____

d. $\dfrac{2}{6}$ and $\dfrac{4}{6}$ _____

e. $\dfrac{1}{10}$ and $\dfrac{9}{10}$ _____

f. $\dfrac{1}{3}$ and $\dfrac{3}{3}$ _____

5 Complete the calculation shown on the number line.

_____ − _____ = _____

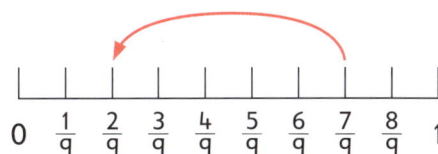

Tip Remember to start the subtraction from the larger number and count back on the number line in ninths to the smaller number.

Apply

6 A large pizza has 12 slices. Maddie eats $\dfrac{3}{12}$ and Noah eats 4 slices. What fraction of the whole pizza is left? _____

7 The number in each block is the sum of the numbers in the two blocks below it. Write the missing fractions in the blocks.

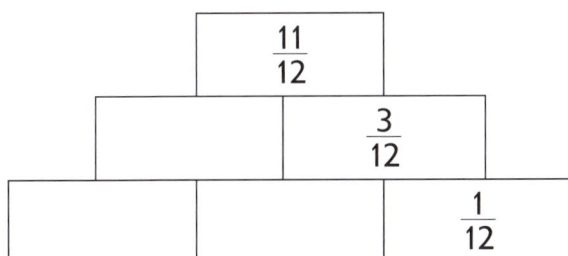

Tip Subtract the fraction in the lower block from the fraction in the block above it. This will find the fraction missing from the block next to it.

Length

Remember

Length is the distance from one end of something to the other end. Length is measured in metres (m), centimetres (cm) and millimetres (mm). Always start measuring from 0 on a ruler. For example: the length of this line is 6cm. Check with a ruler.

When adding or subtracting lengths, change the measurements so that they are in the same units first. For example: 2m + 2cm = 200cm + 2cm = 202cm

Practise

1. Measure the length of each line using a ruler and write it to the nearest cm.

    a. _____   _____

    b. _____   _____

    c. _____   _____

2. Draw **two** lines that are greater than 8cm and **two** lines that are less than 6cm.

3. Circle the best estimate for each of these items.

    a. the height of a cereal box   40mm   40cm   40m   400cm

    b. the length of a pencil   13mm   13cm   13m   130cm

    c. the height of a door   2mm   2cm   2m   20cm

    d. the length of a bee   15mm   15cm   15m   150cm

Tip There are 100cm in 1m and 1000mm in 1m. There are 10mm in 1cm.

⟫ Extend

4 Add these lengths.

  a. 36cm + 23cm = _____ cm   **b.** 143cm + 222cm = _____ cm

  c. 356cm + 237cm = _____ cm   **d.** 386cm + 432cm = _____ cm

  e. 656cm + 253cm = _____ cm   **f.** 483cm + 265cm = _____ cm

5 Subtract these lengths.

  a. 36cm − 23cm = _____ cm   **b.** 243cm − 122cm = _____ cm

  c. 456cm − 137cm = _____ cm   **d.** 586cm − 283cm = _____ cm

  e. 645cm − 284cm = _____ cm   **f.** 567cm − 392cm = _____ cm

💭 Apply

6 Write the length of each pencil.

a.

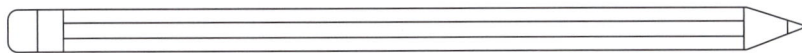
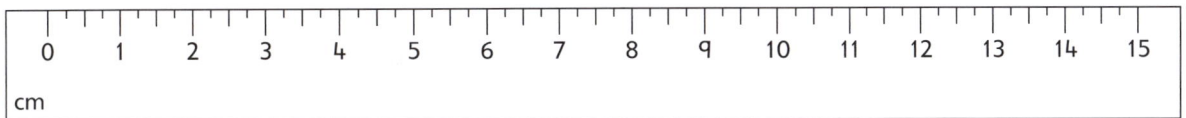

_____

b.

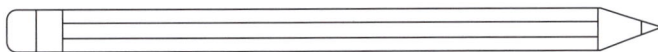
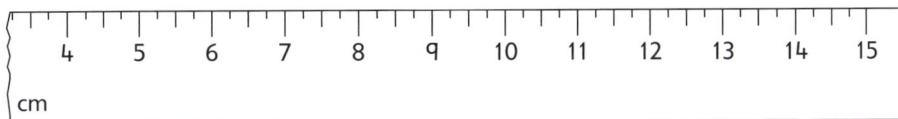

_____

7 Tom and Ashley are skipping. Tom's skipping rope is 2m and 25cm long. Ashley's skipping rope is 205cm long. Circle who has the longest skipping rope. Circle **one**.

Tom   Ashley

Explain your answer.

_____

Perimeter

Remember

Perimeter is the total distance around a shape. To find the perimeter of a rectangle, measure or count the squares of each side of the rectangle and add all the lengths together.

For example: the perimeter of this rectangle is 4cm + 4cm + 2cm + 2cm = 12cm.

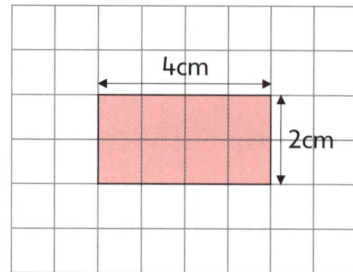

Practise

1. These rectangles have been drawn on a centimetre square grid. Count the squares to find the perimeter of each rectangle.

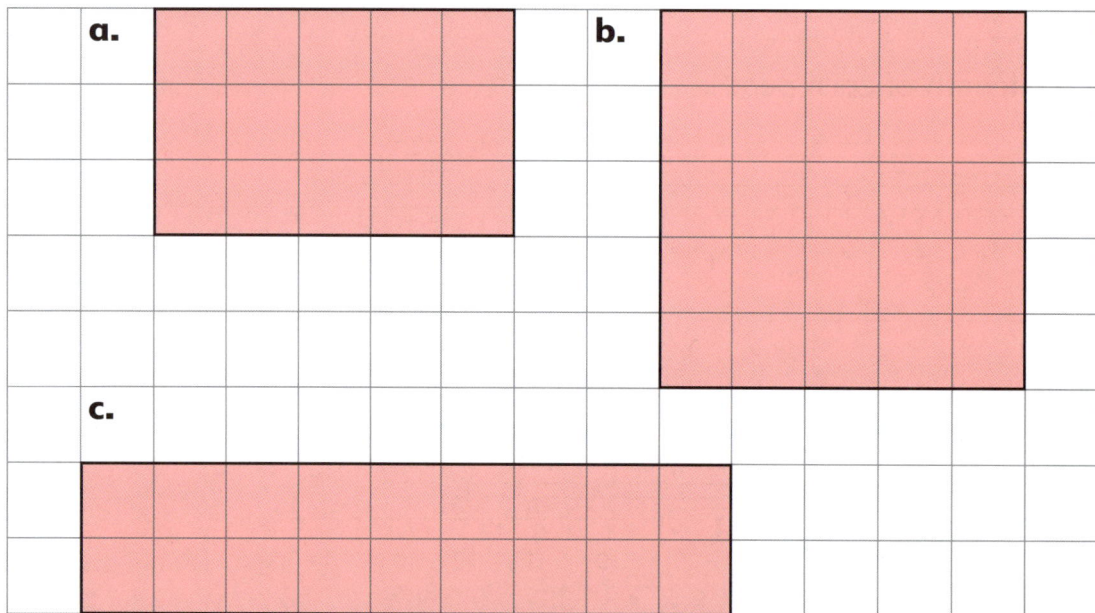

a. _____   b. _____   c. _____

2. Calculate the perimeters of these shapes.

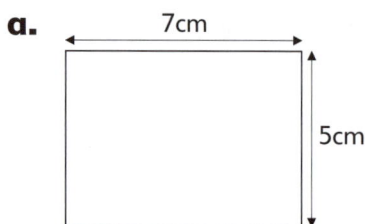 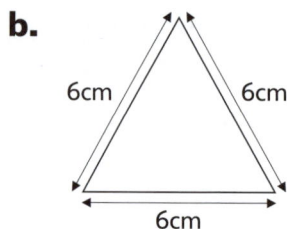 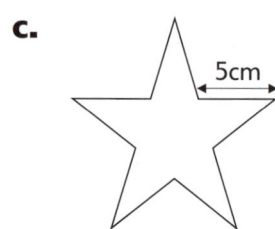

_____   _____   _____

3 Measure the sides of each shape to work out their perimeters.

a.

b.

_____   _____

4 Complete this table to show the lengths, widths and perimeters of these rectangles.

	Length	Width	Perimeter
a.	15cm	6cm	
b.	22cm	10cm	
c.	30cm		100cm

Apply

5 Susie has drawn two regular shapes. Use the perimeter to calculate the length of each side of the regular shape.

a. perimeter = 72cm   **b.** perimeter = 72cm

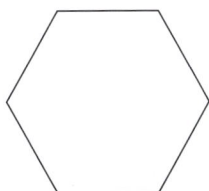   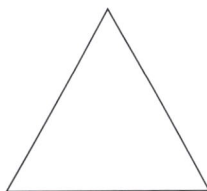

Tip A regular shape has equal-length sides.

_____   _____

Mass

Remember

The mass of an object shows how much of something there is and how much it weighs. The units kilograms (kg) and grams (g) are used most often when measuring mass. There are 1000 grams in 1 kilogram. When adding or subtracting masses, make sure to convert the units so that they are both the same first.

Practise

1. Write the unit of measurement that would be most likely used to measure each of the following. Write kg or g.

   a. an orange _____   **b.** a suitcase _____   **c.** a bar of chocolate _____

2. Write the mass of each parcel. Include the correct units.

   a.
   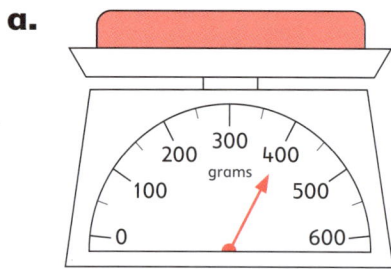
   _____

   b.

   _____

   c.
   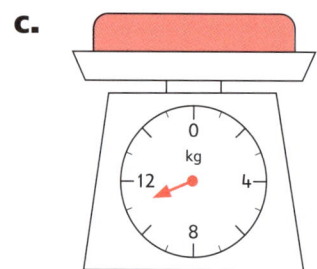
   _____

3. Draw the arrow on the scale to show the mass of each parcel.

   a.
   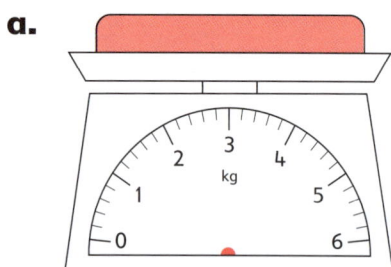
   3kg

   b.
   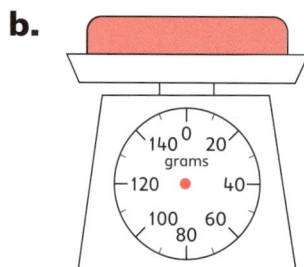
   130g

   c.
   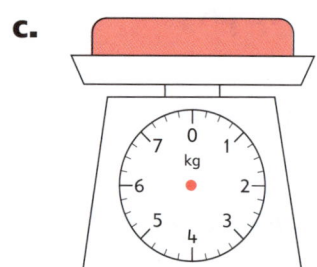
   4.5kg

Tip Look carefully at the divisions on the scale. Some divisions are numbered and some are not.

4 Add these masses.

a. 73g + 23g = _____ g

b. 256g + 27g = _____ g

c. 168kg + 325kg = _____ kg

d. 346kg + 47kg = _____ kg

e. 679g + 62g = _____ g

f. 562g + 45g = _____ g

g. 456g + 353g = _____ g

h. 284g + 567g = _____ g

Tip It might help to change between kg and g when adding and subtracting.
1 kilogram = 1000g

5 Subtract these masses.

a. 65g − 23g = _____ g

b. 323g − 172g = _____ g

c. 278kg − 184kg = _____ kg

d. 673kg − 92kg = _____ kg

e. 875g − 62g = _____ g

f. 436g − 55g = _____ g

g. 782g − 537g = _____ g

h. 409g − 264g = _____ g

Apply

6 Lara buys some potatoes. They have a mass of 975g.
She uses 595g to make a fish pie. What is the mass of
potatoes that is left?

_____

7 Calculate the difference between the masses of these two bags of sugar.

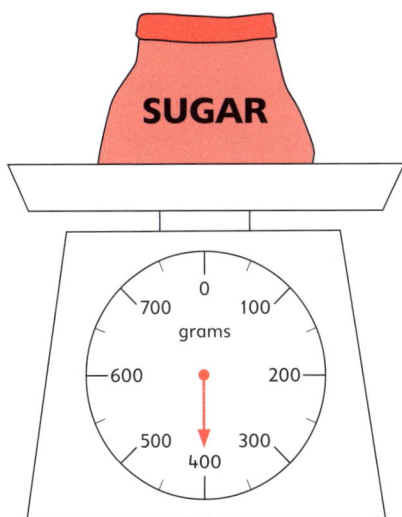

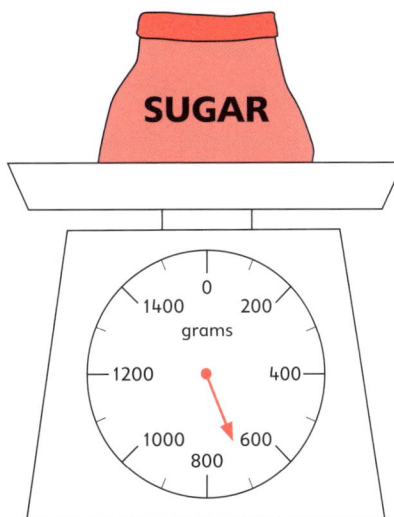

_____

Capacity

Remember

The capacity is the amount of liquid a container holds. The units litres (l) and millilitres (ml) are used when measuring capacity. There are 1000 millilitres in 1 litre. When adding or subtracting capacity, make sure to convert the units so that they are both the same first.

Practise

1 Write the unit of measurement that would be most likely used to measure each of the following. Write l or ml.

a. a teacup _____   **b.** a kettle _____   **c.** a can of drink _____

2 Write the amount of water in each jug. Include the correct units.

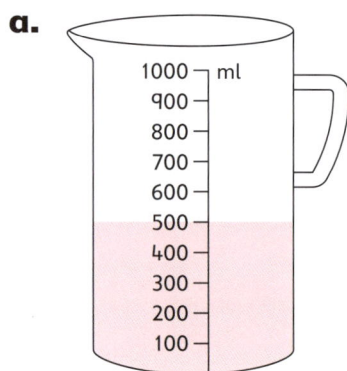

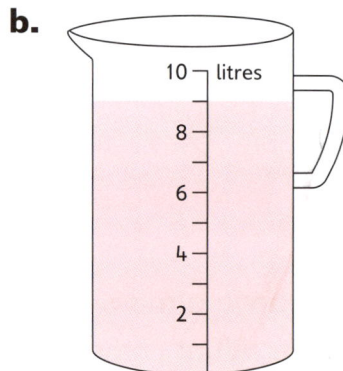

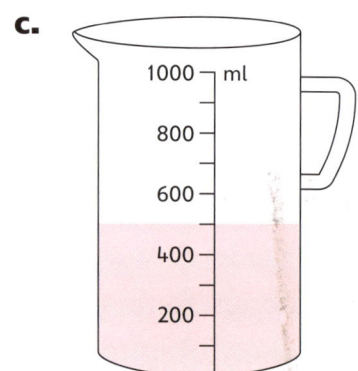

a.

```
1000 ┐ ml
 900 ┤
 800 ┤
 700 ┤
 600 ┤
 500 ┤
 400 ┤
 300 ┤
 200 ┤
 100 ┤
```

b.

```
10 ┐ litres
 8 ┤
 6 ┤
 4 ┤
 2 ┤
```

c.

```
1000 ┐ ml
 800 ┤
 600 ┤
 400 ┤
 200 ┤
```

_____   _____   _____

3 Draw a line to show how much water is in each jug.

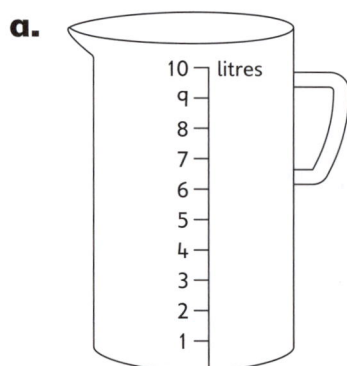

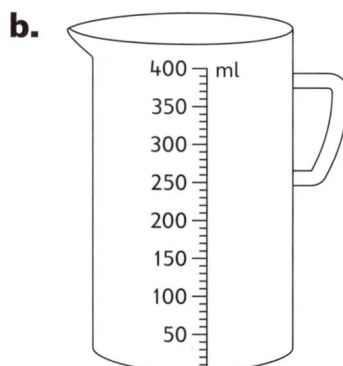

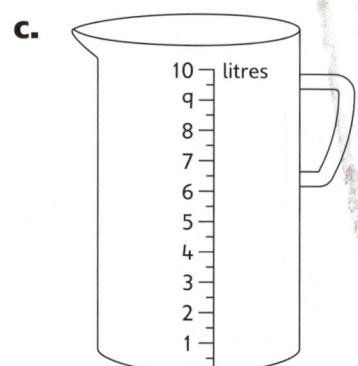

a.

```
10 ┐ litres
 9 ┤
 8 ┤
 7 ┤
 6 ┤
 5 ┤
 4 ┤
 3 ┤
 2 ┤
 1 ┤
```

5 litres

b.

```
400 ┐ ml
350 ┤
300 ┤
250 ┤
200 ┤
150 ┤
100 ┤
 50 ┤
```

320ml

c.

```
10 ┐ litres
 9 ┤
 8 ┤
 7 ┤
 6 ┤
 5 ┤
 4 ┤
 3 ┤
 2 ┤
 1 ┤
```

3.5 litres

4   Add these capacities.

   a. 84ml + 32ml = _____ ml   **b.** 342ml + 246ml = _____ ml

   c. 265ml + 354ml = _____ ml   **d.** 472ml + 509ml = _____ ml

   e. 534ml + 62ml = _____ ml   **f.** 285ml + 75ml = _____ ml

   g. 654ml + 354ml = _____ ml   **h.** 810ml + 385ml = _____ ml

Tip It might help to change between l and ml when adding and subtracting.
1l = 1000ml

5   Subtract these capacities.

   a. 73ml − 34ml = _____ ml   **b.** 152 ml − 101ml = _____ ml

   c. 473ml − 292ml = _____ ml   **d.** 543ml − 185ml = _____ ml

   e. 645ml − 35ml = _____ ml   **f.** 705ml − 68ml = _____ ml

   g. 258ml − 194ml = _____ ml   **h.** 510ml − 325ml = _____ ml

 Apply

6   Hiran is making a drink. He pours 125ml of fruit squash
into a glass and adds 255ml of water. How many millilitres
of drink are in the glass?   _____

7   Here is a jug of water.

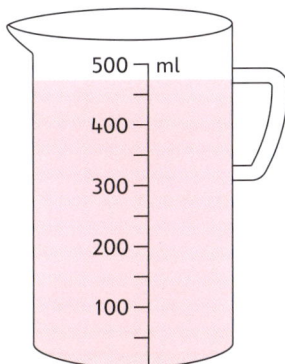

Tip Use the intervals
(spaces) between the
numbers on the scale
to work out the amount
of water in the jug.

Beth pours 225 millilitres of water out of the jug. How
much water will be left in the jug?   _____

Mixed measurements

Remember

These questions practise the measurements learnt so far. Use the following information to answer the questions.

Length measures how long something is from one end to the other. Length is measured in millimetres, centimetres and metres.

Mass measures how much of something there is. Mass is measured in kilograms and grams.

Capacity is how much liquid a container holds. Capacity is measured in litres and millilitres.

Practise

1 Use the letters to order the fruits from heaviest to lightest.

78g	96g	72g	99g	74g
		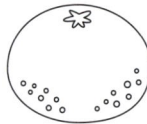		
A	**B**	**C**	**D**	**E**

2 Measure the lines and write the measurements in order from shortest to longest.

A ——————————————

B ——————————————————

C ————————

D ——————————————

E ————————————————————

Tip Make sure 0cm on the ruler lines up with one end of the line. Read the measurement at the other end of the line.

3 What is the total amount of water in these two jugs?

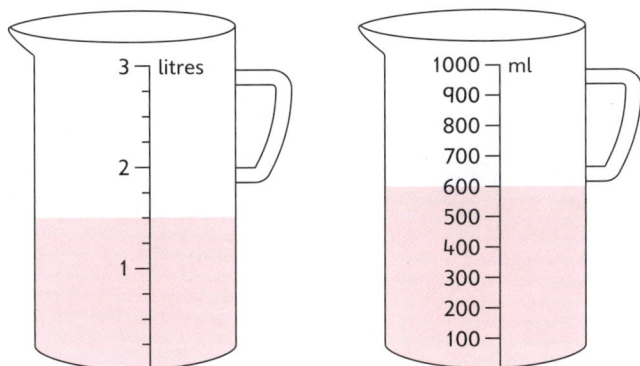

_____

4 Find the missing amounts on these number lines.

a. A

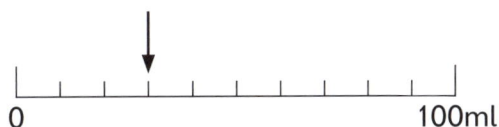

0   100ml

A = _____

b. 300g

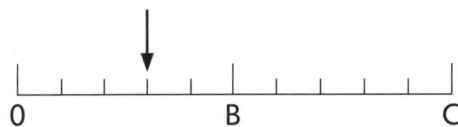

0   B   C

B = _____   C = _____

c. D   E

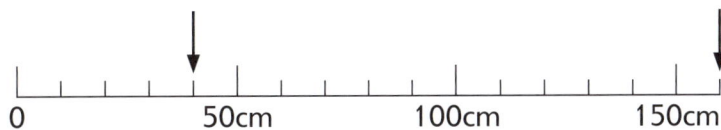

0   50cm   100cm   150cm

D = _____   E = _____

Apply

5 There are 2kg of flour in the bag. Eliza uses 1kg 200g
to bake bread. How much flour is left in the bag?   _____

6 Leo needs 1 litre of water. He has two jugs filled with water as shown.

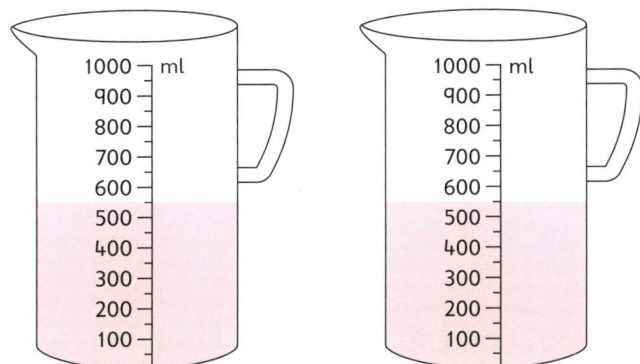

How much extra water does he have?   _____

Time language and facts

bnstx3

Remember

Time measures how long something takes. The units for time are seconds, minutes, hours, days, months and years. There are 60 seconds in a minute, 60 minutes in an hour, 24 hours in a day and 365 days in a year (or 366 days in a leap year).

Practise

1 Complete the sentences using these time words.

| day   afternoon   morning   a.m.   p.m.   night   midnight   midday |

a. _____ refers to the time when there is daylight and

_____ refers to the time when it is dark.

b. The times from 12 midnight to 12 _____ are called

_____ times.

c. The times from 12 midday to 12 _____ are called

_____ times.

d. _____ is the time between sunrise and midday.

e. _____ is the time between midday and sunset.

Tip a.m. means 'before noon' and p.m. means 'after noon'.

2 Ali says that there is another way to say midday. Is Ali correct? Circle **one**.

Yes   No

Explain your answer.

_____

3 Fill in the missing numbers.

a. There are _____ months in a year.

b. There are _____ seconds in a minute.

c. There are _____ hours in a day.

d. There are _____ days in a year that is not a leap year.

4 Put these months in order from fewest to greatest number of days. If two months have the same number of days, put them in the order they come in the year.

a. September, February, July

_____

b. October, April, January

_____

Apply

5 Solve these problems.

a. It is 18th January in a leap year. How many days are left in the year? _____

b. There are 32 days until the end of the year. What is the date? _____

Tip The number of days left in the year does not include today.

6 Josh says that a leap year is every 6 years and this is when February has 30 days. Is Josh correct? Circle **one**.

Yes   No

Explain your answer.

_____

_____

Telling the time

Remember

An analogue clock usually has the numbers 1 to 12 around its face. A digital clock displays the time in numbers. Time can be shown using 12-hour or 24-hour times.

12-hour time

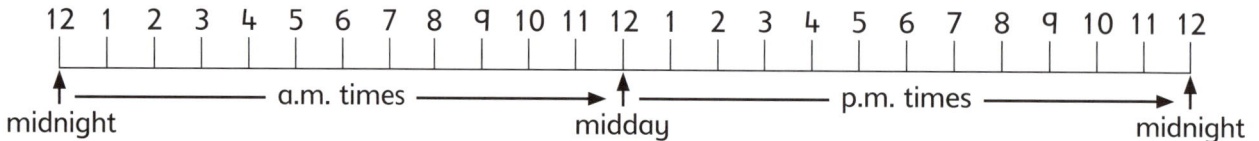

24-hour time

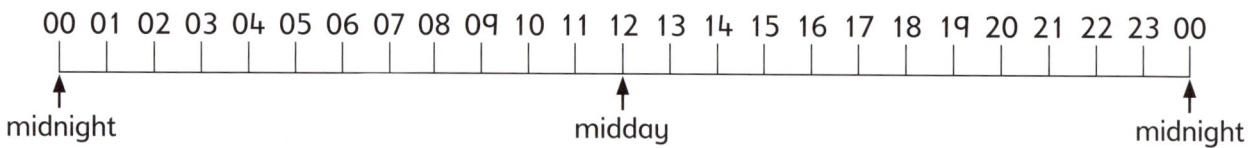

Practise

1) Draw hands on the clocks to show the times. One has been done for you.

a. quarter past 6

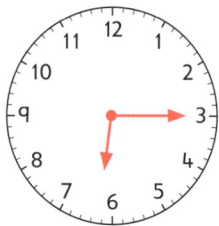

b. half past 8

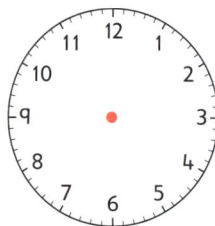

c. 9 o'clock

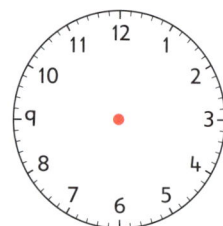

d. 20 minutes past 4

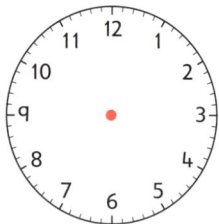

e. 5 minutes to 7

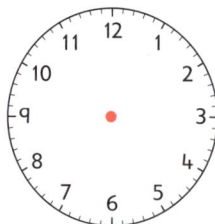

f. 13 minutes past 8

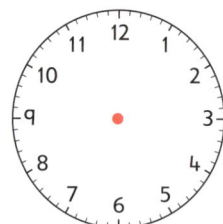

2) Write the time shown on the digital clock in words. One has been done for you.

a. 06:30

   half past 6

_____

b. 11:15

_____

_____

c. 10:12

_____

_____

3) Write the times shown by these clocks in 12-hour time.

a.

an evening time

_____

b.

a morning time

_____

c.

an afternoon time

_____

Tip Use a.m. with 12-hour times before midday and p.m. with 12-hour times after midday.

4) Write the times shown by these clocks in 24-hour time.

a.

a morning time

_____

b.
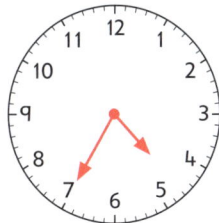
an afternoon time

_____

c.

a night time

_____

Tip Make sure you always use four digits when you write 24-hour times.

Apply

5) Here are four clocks. It is Sunday at midday.

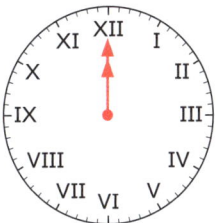
A

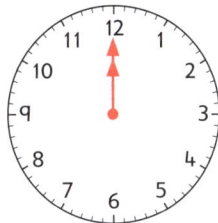
B

| 12:00 |
C

| 00:00 |
D

Devi says one clock is **not** correct. Explain which clock is **not** correct.

_____

Time problems

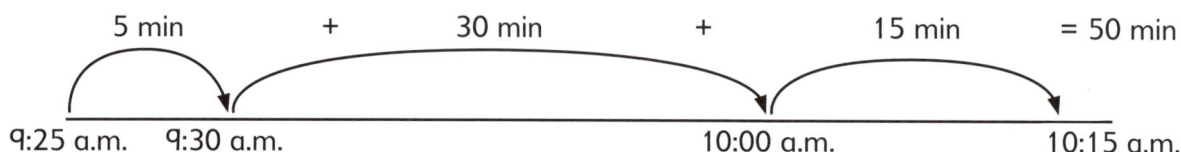
Practise

1 Write the length of time that has passed between the two clocks.

a.

   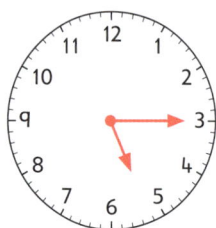

afternoon   afternoon

_____

b.

morning   morning

_____

c.

| 10:30 | 12:45 |

_____

d.

| 13:35 | 17:00 |

_____

2 Write the correct symbol (<, > or =) in the circle to compare the times.

a. 60 seconds ◯ 2 minutes

b. 365 days ◯ a leap year

c. days in April ◯ days in September

d. 48 hours ◯ 1 day

e. 10 months ◯ 1 year

f. a fortnight ◯ 1 week

Tip Convert one of the times so that they both use the same units. When they are both in the same units, you will be able to compare them easily.

3 Sam starts school at 9:00 a.m.

   a. He has his lunch $3\frac{1}{2}$ hours after school starts. Show what time he has lunch on the 12-hour digital clock.

:

   b. He has an art lesson 4 hours after school starts. Show what time he has his art lesson on the 24-hour digital clock.

:

4 These are the fees displayed at the car park.

Up to 20 minutes	50p
21 to 45 minutes	£1
More than 45 minutes	£1 and 10p

Tip Read the table carefully to answer the problems.

   a. Oscar leaves his car at 11:25 a.m. and has paid £1. What time must he return to his car? _____

   b. Meg parks from 14:35 to 15:10. How much does Meg pay for parking? _____

Apply

5 Tim wants to eat his dinner at 18:30. His pizza takes 18 minutes to cook. Tim says that he must put the pizza in the oven at 18:48. Is Tim correct? Circle **one**.

Yes   No

Explain your answer.

_____

6 Taj practises his trumpet three days each week. On Monday, he starts at 17:09 and finishes at 17:21. On Wednesday, he starts at 18:49 and finishes at 19:02. On Saturday, he starts at 10:45 a.m. and finishes at 11:23 a.m. On which day does Taj practise the longest? _____

Money problems

Remember

Money uses the units pounds and pence. 100p = £1. There are eight coins used in the money system:

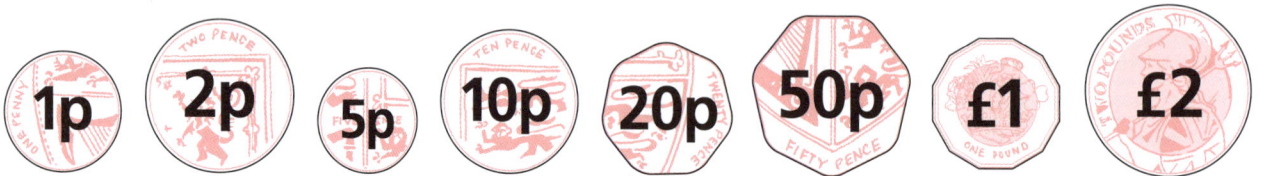

1p 2p 5p 10p 20p 50p £1 £2

Practise

1 Write the amount of money shown.

a.
20p 20p 20p 20p
20p 50p 50p

_____

b.
£1 £1 £1
50p 50p

_____

c.
£2 10p 10p 10p 10p 10p
10p 10p 10p 10p 10p

_____

d.
5p 5p 5p 5p
50p 10p 10p 10p

_____

2 Write the correct symbol (<, > or =) in the circle to compare the amounts of money.

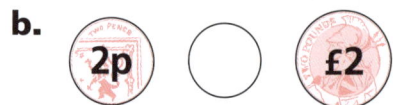

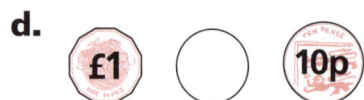

a. 10p 10p 10p 10p ◯ £1

b. 2p ◯ £2

c. £2 ◯ 50p 50p 50p 50p

d. £1 ◯ 10p

e. 5p 5p 5p 5p ◯ 20p

f. 50p ◯ 5p

>> Extend

3 These bar models represent addition and subtraction calculations. Find the missing amounts.

a.

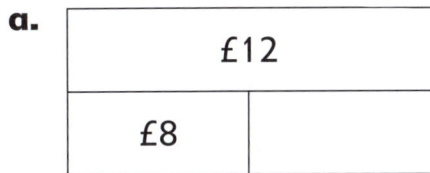

£12	
£8	

b.

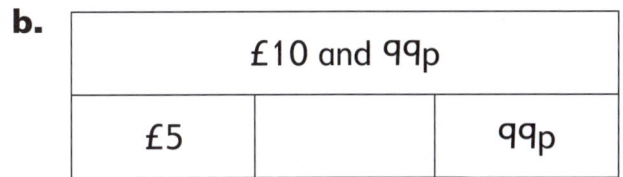

£10 and 99p		
£5		99p

4 Here are the prices of items for sale at the beach shop.

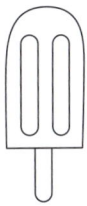  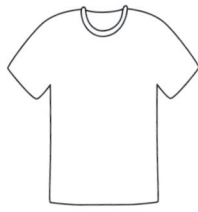  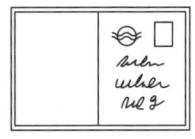

45p   £3 and 75p   £6   £2 and 40p   £1 and 20p   35p

Calculate the cost and change from £10 for each of these sets of items.

a.

Cost: _____

Change: _____

b.

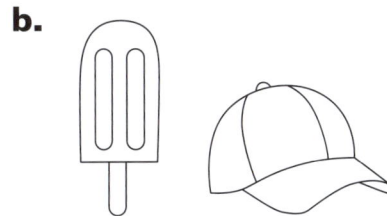

Cost: _____

Change: _____

⚬ Apply

5 This table shows the prices for tickets to an aquarium.

a. What is the price for 1 adult and 2 children?

_____

b. How much will 2 adults and 2 children save if they buy a group ticket rather than individual tickets?

_____

Ticket	Price
Adult	£12
Child	£7 and 50p
Group (2 adults + 2 children)	£30

Lines

Remember

There are different types of lines:

horizontal lines   vertical lines   perpendicular lines   parallel lines

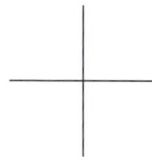

Perpendicular lines cross at right angles. Parallel lines go in the same direction and never cross.

✏ Practise

1 Count the number of vertical and horizontal lines in this picture.

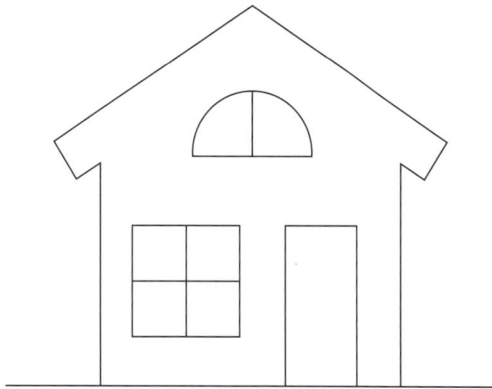

Tip It might help to tick each line as you count it to make sure you only count each line once.

There are _____ vertical lines and _____ horizontal lines.

2 Circle the letter in each word that has a pair of parallel lines.

a. H O T   b. Z O O   c. B U N   d. F O X

3 Draw an example of each type of line in its box.

Vertical line	Horizontal line	Parallel lines	Perpendicular lines

⟫ Extend

4 Write how many pairs of parallel lines there are in each shape.

a.  _____

b. 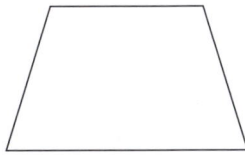 _____

c.  _____

d. 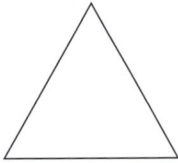 _____

e. 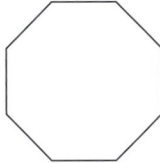 _____

f. 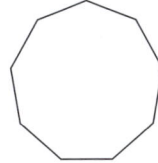 _____

💭 Apply

5 Write the letters in the correct part of the Venn diagram.

| M   E   F   H   L   T   S |

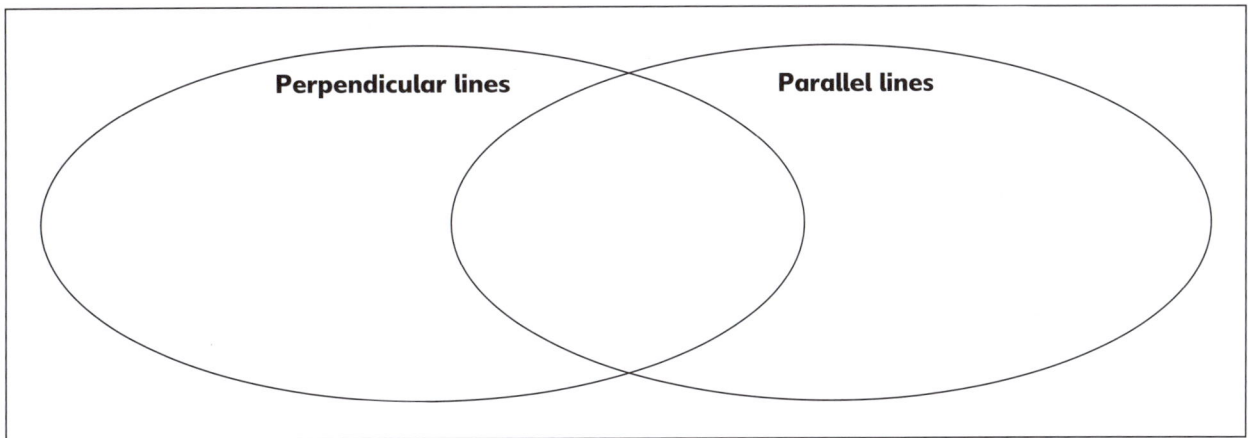

6 This is a sorting diagram for 2D shapes. Write the missing titles from the box in the correct place on the sorting diagram.

| Parallel lines   No parallel lines   Perpendicular lines   No perpendicular lines |

2D shapes

Remember

A 2D shape is a flat shape with two dimensions – length and width. 2D shapes that have straight sides are called polygons. Identify a 2D shape by counting the number of sides and vertices (corners). Examples of 2D shapes include squares, rectangles, triangles, pentagons, hexagons and octagons.

Practise

1 Draw these 2D shapes.

a. square

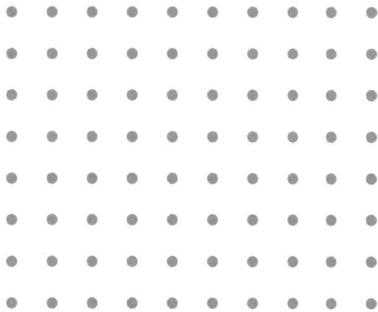

b. rectangle

c. triangle

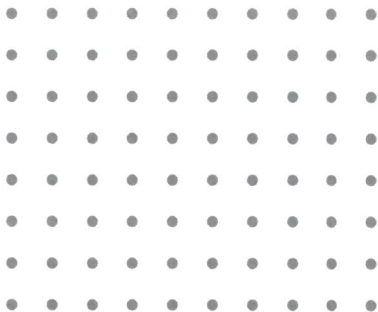

d. pentagon

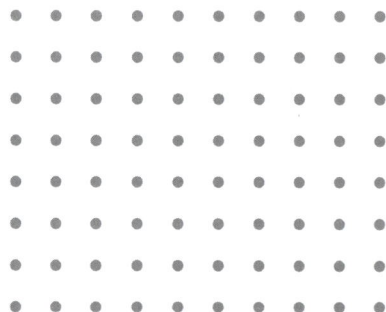

2 Complete the table to show the number of vertices and sides for each shape.

	Shape		Vertices	Sides
a.	Octagon			
b.	Parallelogram			
c.	Kite			

Tip Vertices are the corners of the shape.

3 Write the name of each shape.

a.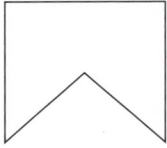

b.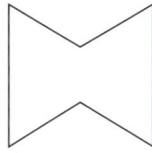

c.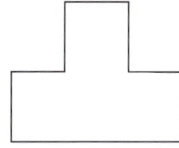

_____   _____   _____

4 One shape has **not** been placed correctly on the sorting diagram.

Write the letter of the shape that is **not** in the correct place.

_____

Explain your answer.

Octagons		Not octagons	
A	⬡	D	✶
B	⬡	E	⇨
C	✕	F	⚡

_____

Apply

5 Syed puts these shapes into order from the smallest number of sides to the largest number of sides.

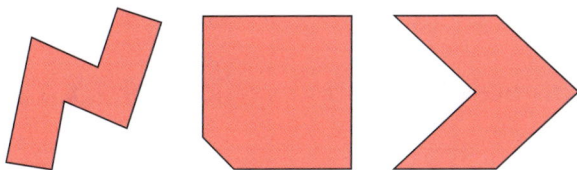

Write the name of the 2D shape that will come last.

_____

6 Zara want to put all these shapes into a box and label the box 'polygons'.

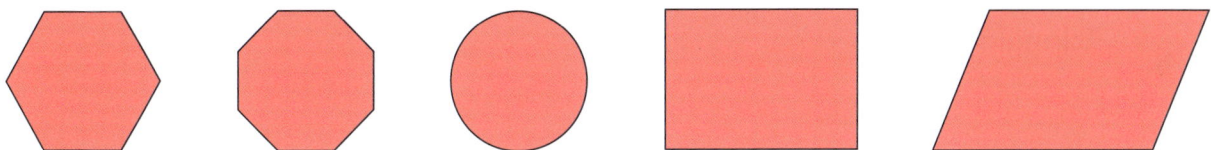

Explain why Zara is **not** able to do this.

_____

3D shapes

Practise

(1) Write the name of each 3D shape.

a.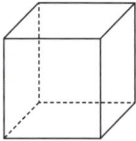

_____

_____

b.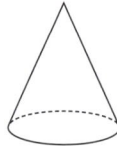

_____

_____

c.

_____

_____

d.

_____

_____

e.

_____

_____

f.

_____

_____

(2) Complete this table to show the number of faces, edges and vertices for each shape.

	Shape		Faces	Edges	Vertices
a.	Cube	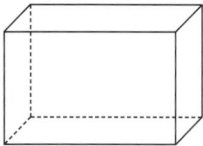			
b.	Triangle-based pyramid				
c.	Triangular prism	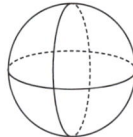			

Tip The edges of a 3D shape are where two faces of the shape meet.

>> Extend

3 Mason is doing 3D shape printing. He prints the shapes from the faces of different 3D shapes. Write the names of the 3D shapes that the faces make when they are put together.

a.

_____

b.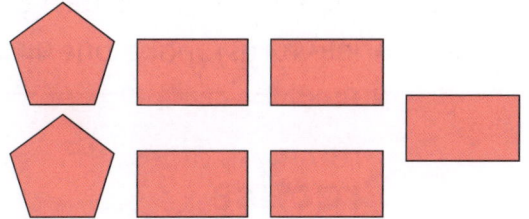

_____

Apply

4 Amira wants to make a cube using spaghetti strands and marshmallows. She will use spaghetti strands for the edges of the cube and marshmallows for the vertices. How many spaghetti strands and how many marshmallows does Amira need?

_____ spaghetti strands and _____ marshmallows

5 Here are some shapes. Andy says that all the shapes are 3D shapes and they are all prisms.

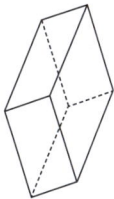 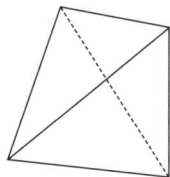 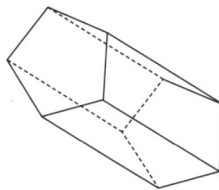 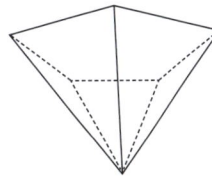 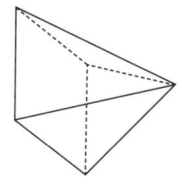

  A   **B**   **C**   **D**   **E**

Is Andy correct? Circle **one**.

Yes   No

Explain your answer.

_____

_____

_____

Turns

Remember

An angle is a description of a turn. An angle is formed when two straight lines meet. A right angle is a quarter turn and is equal to 90 degrees (90°). Four quarter turns (right-angle turns) make one whole (full) turn.

✏️ Practise

1. The hand on the spinner points to 12. Write the number the hand will point to after each of these turns.

   a. a quarter turn clockwise   _____

   b. a half turn anticlockwise   _____

   c. a three-quarter turn clockwise   _____

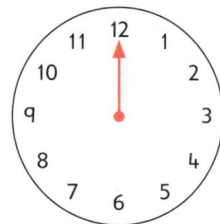

Tip   Turns can be made in two directions, either clockwise or anticlockwise. 'Clockwise' is the direction that the hands move around a clock. 'Anticlockwise' is the opposite direction.

2. Circle the letters of any right angles.

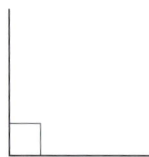 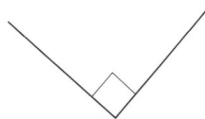  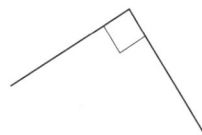

      A   B   C   D   E

3. Use numbers to complete the sentences.

   a. _____ right angle makes a quarter turn.

   b. _____ right angles make a half turn.

   c. _____ right angles make a three-quarter turn.

   d. _____ right angles make a full turn.

Extend

4 Write the correct symbol (<, > or =) in the circle to compare the two angles or turns.

   a. 90° ( ) right angle   **b.** 100° ( ) right angle

   c. 25° ( ) right angle   **d.** 180° ( ) 2 right angles

   e. 360° ( ) full turn   **f.** 180° ( ) half turn

5 Write the letter of each shape in the correct column in the table.

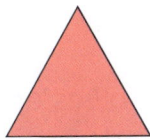 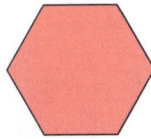 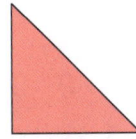 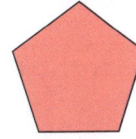 

    A   B   C   D   E   F

Only right angles	Some right angles	No right angles

Apply

6 Here is a compass. Write how many right-angle turns clockwise each direction change is.

   a. north to west   _____

   b. south to north   _____

   c. east to south   _____

   d. west to south   _____

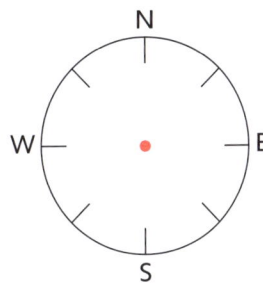

Tip It might help to draw the arrow on to the compass lightly in its starting position. Then count around the compass in right-angle turns until you reach the end position. Make sure you go in a clockwise direction.

Tables

Remember

Tables record information that has been collected. There are different kinds of tables that can be used to show information. Always read the titles and labels carefully to find out the topic of the information in the table.

Practise

1. The school hockey team has been playing matches against other local school hockey teams. Here are the number of goals they scored in their matches.

| 1 | 2 | 1 | 0 | 1 | 2 | 2 | 2 | 1 | 0 | 0 | 4 | 1 |
| 1 | 1 | 1 | 1 | 1 | 2 | 2 | 3 | 2 | 1 | 1 | 3 |

Tip Tallies are marked in groups of five. ⅢⅠ

Number of goals	Tally	Frequency
0		
1		
2		
3		
4		

a. Complete the tally chart to show the number of goals.

b. In how many matches did the team score 1 goal? _____

c. In how many matches did the team score 4 goals? _____

d. What number of goals per match is the most frequent? _____

e. In how many more matches did they score 1 goal than 2 goals? _____

Tip The phrase 'is the most frequent' means 'happens most often'.

Extend

2 This table shows the number of children attending the different swimming level classes at the swimming club.

Tadpoles	Frogs	Dolphins	Sharks
178	234	195	138

a. How many more children are in Frogs than Tadpoles? _____

b. Tadpoles has space for 220 children. How many more spaces are available? _____

3 This table shows the number of visitors to the local art gallery last weekend.

	Saturday	Sunday
Adults	268	345
Children		275
Total	405	

a. How many adults and children visited the art gallery on Sunday?

_____

b. How many children visited the art gallery on Saturday? _____

Apply

4 This table shows the different types of birds visiting a bird table. Complete the table using these clues.

a. One fewer starlings than robins visited the bird table in the morning.

b. Two times as many wrens visited the bird table in the afternoon as in the morning.

c. A quarter of the number of sparrows that visited the bird table in the morning visited in the afternoon.

d. A third of the number of robins that visited the bird table in the morning visited in the afternoon.

	Morning	Afternoon
Wren	6	
Robin	3	
Sparrow	12	
Blackbird		6
Starling		3
Total	25	

Bar charts

Remember

A bar chart is a kind of graph that uses bars or blocks to represent information. The bars can be drawn vertically or horizontally. They are drawn against two axes. One axis will state what each bar is showing and the other axis will give information about the quantities involved.

Practise

1. A youth football club has a tournament every Saturday. This bar chart shows the number of times each team in the club has won the tournament.

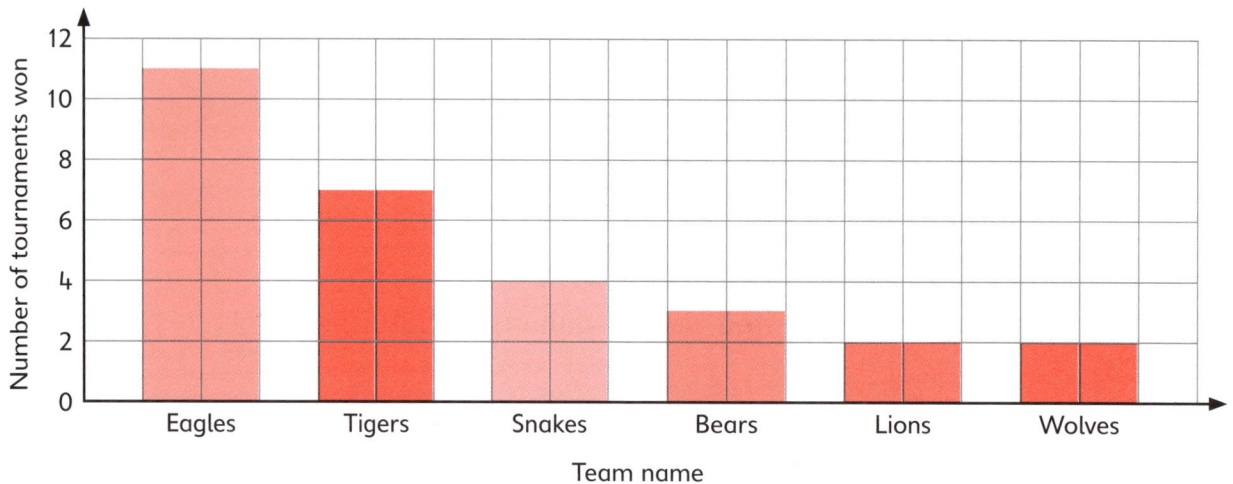

a. How many tournaments have the Snakes won? _____

b. How many tournaments have the Tigers won? _____

c. Who has won the greatest number of tournaments? _____

d. What is the combined number of tournaments that the Lions and the Wolves have won together? _____

e. How many more tournaments have the Tigers won than the Lions? _____

f. What is the total number of tournaments won by all six football teams? _____

Tip When a bar is half-way between two numbers on the scale, it is showing the number that is half-way between those two numbers.

(2) A school magazine asked adults and children whether Year 3 children should get pocket money.

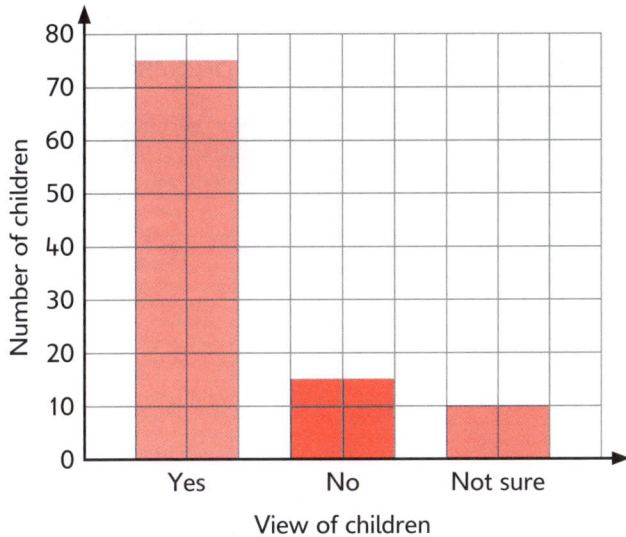

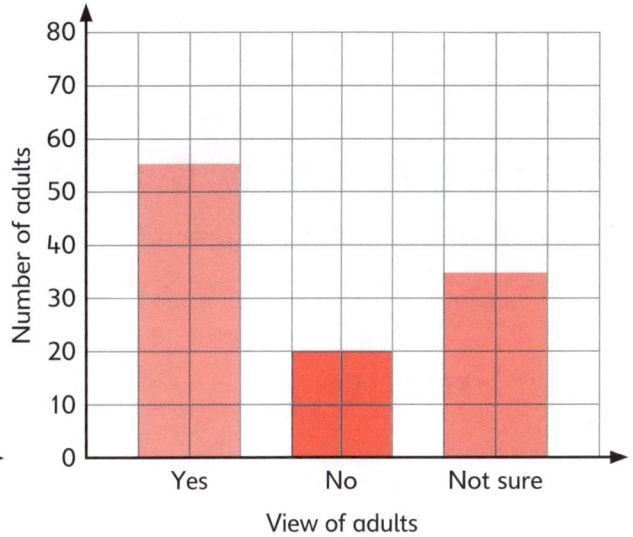

Complete the sentences.

a. _____ children were not sure.

b. _____ adults voted no.

c. _____ more children voted yes compared with adults.

d. _____ adults and children voted in total.

Apply

(3) This bar chart shows the number of items recycled in one week by pupils in Year 3. Complete the bar chart using the information given.

a. There were 75 batteries and items of plastic recycled in total.

b. There were 5 times as many cardboard items recycled as the number of batteries.

c. 215 items were recycled altogether.

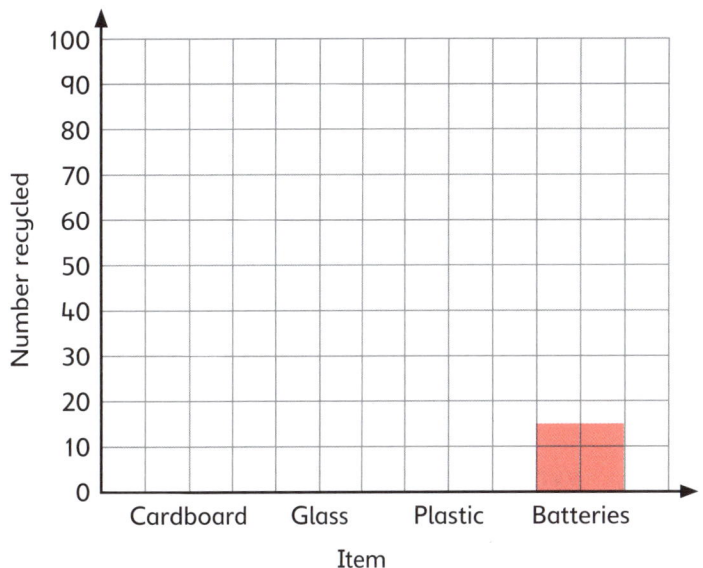

Pictograms

Practise

1. This pictogram shows the money Kate earnt during the summer holiday by helping out at the local café.

Week	Amount earnt
Week 1	£ £ £ £ £
Week 2	£ £ £ £ £ £ £
Week 3	£ £ £ £
Week 4	£ £ £ £ £ £ £
Week 5	£ £ £ £ £ £ £ £ £ £
Week 6	£ £ £ £

£ = £4

a. How much money did Kate earn in week 1? _____

b. Which week did Kate earn the most amount of money? _____

c. How much more money did Kate earn in week 2 than in week 6? _____

d. Kate spent $\frac{1}{4}$ of the money she earnt in week 3 on a magazine. How much did the magazine cost? _____

e. It was Kate's birthday in week 6, so she received an extra £10. How much money did she receive in total in week 6? _____

f. In week 5, how much more money did Kate need to earn to have earnt £50? _____

2 This pictogram shows the number of visitors at tourist attractions in a city on Friday.

Attraction	Number of visitors
Castle	𝑥 𝑥 𝑥 𝑥 𝑥 𝑥 𝑥 𝑥 𝑥 𝑥 𝑥
Zoo	𝑥 𝑥 𝑥 𝑥 𝑥 𝑥 𝑥 𝑥 𝑥 𝑥 𝑥 𝑥 𝑥 𝑥 𝑥 ⸯ
Bridge	𝑥 𝑥 𝑥 𝑥 𝑥 𝑥 𝑥 𝑥 𝑥 𝑥 𝑥 𝑥 𝑥 𝑥 𝑥 𝑥 𝑥 𝑥
Bus tour	𝑥 𝑥 𝑥 𝑥 𝑥 𝑥 𝑥 𝑥 𝑥 𝑥 𝑥 ⸯ
Museum	𝑥 𝑥 𝑥 𝑥 𝑥 𝑥 𝑥

𝑥 = 50 tourists

a. How many tourists visited the castle? _____

b. How many more tourists visited the zoo than the museum? _____

c. $\frac{1}{10}$ of the tourists that visited the bridge are over the age of 70. How many people over the age of 70 visited the bridge? _____

d. Lucy says only 7 people visited the museum. Explain why Lucy is **not** correct.

_____

Apply

3 This pictogram shows the number of tiles made at three different factories.

Factory	Number of tiles
Factory 1	▦ ▦ ▦ ▦ ▦ ▦ ▪
Factory 2	▦ ▦ ▦ ▦ ▦ ▦ ▦ ▪
Factory 3	▦ ▦ ▦ ▦ ◰

▦ = 100 tiles

a. How many tiles are produced by factory 1? _____

b. How many more tiles are produced by factory 2 than factory 1? _____

c. How many tiles are produced by all three factories? _____

d. Factory 2 was supposed to produce 1000 tiles. How many tiles did they fail to produce? _____

Final practice

The Final practice assesses knowledge from every unit of this book. Work through the questions carefully and try to answer each one. The target time for completing these questions is 45 minutes. The answers can be downloaded from the **Schofield & Sims** website.

1 Zoe has these number cards. List all the three-digit numbers she can make.

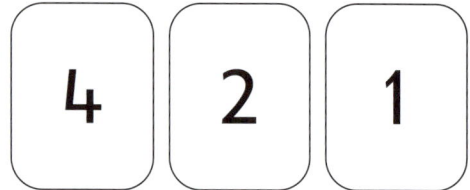

| 4 | 2 | 1 |

2 marks

2 Here is a number sentence. The star is hiding a number.

453 > ★

Circle all the numbers that could be hidden behind the star.

421   534   301   401   468   489   455

1 mark

3 Jenny catches this bus home from school every day. She writes this note down so that she will catch the correct bus:

317

My bus number is three hundred and seventy.

Is Jenny correct? Circle **one**.

Yes   No

Explain your answer.

_____

_____

1 mark

4 Calculate:

a. 495 + 306 = _____

b. 645 − 283 = _____

2 marks

5 Find the missing digits in these calculations.

a.
```
    4 ☐ 7
  +   2 3 2
  ─────────
    6 3 9
```

b.
```
    1   5   4
  +   2   1 ☐
  ───────────
    3   7   2
```

c.
```
    6 ☐ 5
  −   2 6 3
  ─────────
    3 8 2
```
3 marks

6 The table shows the heights of two towers.

Tower A	Tower B
228m	234m

a. What is the combined height of the two towers? _____

b. What is the difference between the heights of the two towers? _____ 2 marks

7 A pack of balloons has 6 green balloons and 4 red balloons. Kwame wants 80 balloons for his grandfather's 80th birthday party. How many packs of balloons does he need to buy? _____ 2 marks

8 Find the missing digits in these calculations.

a.
```
      5 ☐
  ×     3
  ───────
    1 5 9
```

b.
```
      3 ☐
  ×     4
  ───────
  ☐ 4 8
```

c.
```
      6 ☐
  ×     8
  ───────
  4 ☐ 0
```

d.
```
      2 ☐
  ×     8
  ───────
  ☐ 9 2
```
7 marks

9 Some apples are put into bags. 5 apples are put into each bag with 2 apples remaining. There are 16 bags. How many apples were there? _____ 2 marks

10 Fill in the missing numerator and denominator.

$$\frac{}{5} = \frac{8}{}$$

2 marks

11 Naomi, Alex and Lily are thinking about fractions using this sorting diagram.

	Fractions equal to one whole	Fractions less than one whole
Unit fractions		
Non-unit fractions		

Naomi says $\frac{1}{3}$ could be put in the white box. Alex says $\frac{5}{5}$ could be put in the white box. Lily says $\frac{8}{1}$ could be put in the white box. Who is correct?

Explain your answer.

_____

_____

2 marks

12 Here are some shapes.

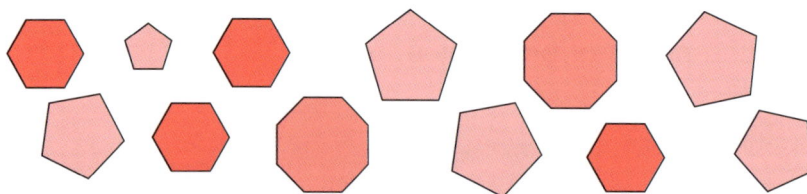

a. What fraction of the shapes are pentagons? _____

b. What fraction of the shapes are octagons? _____

c. What fraction of the shapes are hexagons? _____

3 marks

13 Here is a jug with water in it. Dominic pours $\frac{4}{10}$ of the water out of this jug into a glass. He then pours 150 millilitres of water out of the same jug into another glass. How much water will be left in the jug?

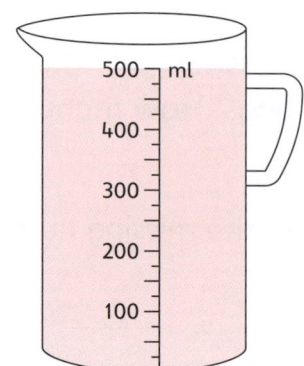

_____

500 ml
400
300
200
100

2 marks

Final practice

14 A gardener joins two hoses together.

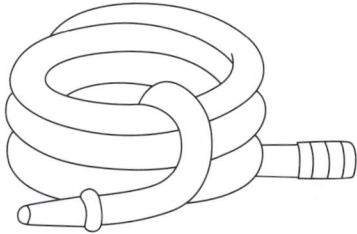 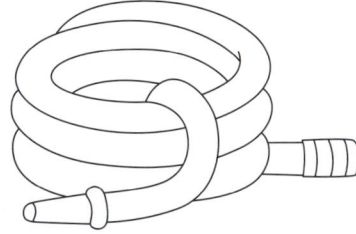

125cm   95cm

a. What is the total length of the combined hose? _____

b. How much more hose needs to be added to
make it 3m long? _____   2 marks

15 Elliot buys a can of drink and a medium box of popcorn at the cinema.

85p   £4 and 65p

He uses a £10 note to pay. How much change does
he get back? _____   2 marks

16 A zookeeper has written down the times of the events at the zoo. She has
used a mixture of 12-hour and 24-hour times. Write the missing times in
the table.

	Event	Start	Length of event	Finish
a.	Feed the penguins	9:20 a.m.	50 min	
b.	Bird of prey show		1 hr 10 min	11:30
c.	Animal arts and crafts	13:45		14:05

3 marks

17 The perimeter of this rectangle is 16cm. What is the length of side A?

_____

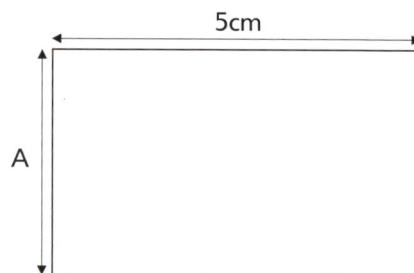

5cm

A

2 marks

18 Here is a bar chart showing the number of drink cartons sold at a drinks stall.

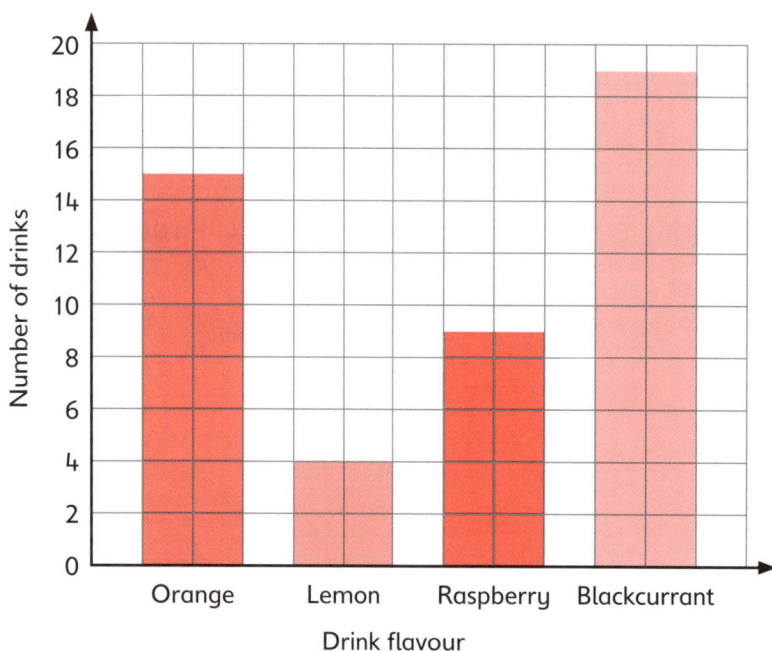

a. How many lemon drink cartons were sold? _____

b. How many raspberry drink cartons were sold? _____

c. How many more blackcurrant than orange drink cartons were sold? _____

d. The drinks stall bought 1 box of 100 drink cartons to sell. How many drink cartons were left? _____

5 marks

Total:

45 marks